ZERO — A MEMORIAL BUILT ON THE SITE OF TREBLINKA, A GERMAN EXTERMINATION CAMP IN POLAND. EACH STONE REPRESENTS A JEWISH TOWN OR CITY, THE POPULATION OF WHICH WAS EXTERMINATED — *ZERO*

ZERO — BOSNIAN PARLIAMENT BUILDING BURNS AFTER BEING HIT BY SERBIAN TANK FIRE (PHOTO BY MIKHAIL EVSTAFIEV) — *ZERO*

ZERO — BOMB SHELTER BY PAUL LASZLO — *ZERO*

ZERO —CHURCHILL EXAMINING DAMAGE IN LONDON AFTER BOMBING, 1944 — *ZERO*

D1458386

ZERO — COMPLEXE DE NEVERS – 'BUNKER CHURCH' BY PAUL VIRILIO AND CLAUDE PARENT, FRANCE, 1966 — *ZERO*

ZERO — DRESDEN AFTER THE ALLIED BOMBING, 1945 — *ZERO*

ZERO — BLOCKHAUS, EPERLECQUES, FRANCE, V2 ROCKETS SITE — *ZERO*

ZERO — HIROSHIMA AFTER THE BOMB, 1945 — *ZERO*

ZERO — THE HOLY LAND EXPERIENCE, ORLANDO, FLORIDA — *ZERO*

ZERO — TEMPLE OF ANGKOR WAT — *ZERO*

ZERO — SHIBAM WADI HADHRAMAUT, YEMEN DESERT — *ZERO*

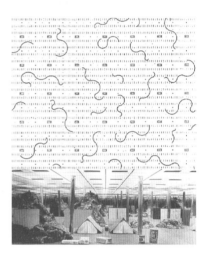

ZERO — NO-STOP CITY/ INTERIOR LANDSCAPE BY ARCHIZOOM, 1969–70 — *ZERO*

ZERO — PLUG-IN CITY, CITY SYNTHESIS BY ARCHIGRAM/ DENNIS CROMPTON, 1963 — *ZERO*

ZERO — SUNSET MOUNTAIN BY CESAR PELLI, 1964 — *ZERO*

ZERO — AVENUE OF THE DEAD TOWARDS THE PYRAMID OF THE MOON AT TEOTIHUACEN — *ZERO*

ZERO — IDEAL CITY CHAUX DE FONDS BY CLAUDE-NICOLAS LEDOUX, 1773 — *ZERO*

ZERO — FOREST CITY BY KIYONORI KIKUTAKE, 1968 — *ZERO*

ZERO — PLAN VOISIN FOR PARIS BY LE CORBUSIER, WITH THE ARCHITECT'S HAND GESTURING TOWARDS THE FUTURE, 1924 — *ZERO*

ZERO — CITY OF THE HEMISPHERES BY SUPERSTUDIO — *ZERO*

ZERO — JERICHO, IN THE WEST BANK, DATES BACK TO 9000 B.C. AND SOME BELIEVE IT IS THE WORLD'S OLDEST CITY — *ZERO*

ZERO — ROADTOWN BY EDGAR CHAMBLESS, 1910 — *ZERO*

ZERO — HOCHHAUSSTADT, LUDWIG HILBERSEIMER, 1924 — *ZERO*

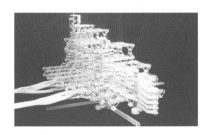

ZERO — RAGNITZ BY EILFRIED HUTH & GÜNTHER DOMENIG — *ZERO*

ZERO — BROADACRE CITY BY FRANK LLOYD WRIGHT, 1932–59 — *ZERO*

ZERO — DISNEYLAND POSTCARD — *ZERO*

ZERO — TOWER OF BABEL BY PIETER BRUEGEL THE ELDER, 1563, MUSEUM BOYMANS-VAN BEUNINGEN, ROTTERDAM — *ZERO*

ZERO — THE CITY BY HANS HOLLEIN, 1960 — *ZERO*

ZERO — CITY OF THE FUTURE BY ROBERT CRUMB, 1975 — *ZERO*

ZERO — PROPOSED NEW PLAN OF LONDON BY CHRISTOPHER WREN, 1666, AFTER THE GREAT FIRE — *ZERO*

ZERO — FORT BOYARD, STARTED UNDER NAPOLEON IN 1801 — *ZERO*

ZERO — DUTCH PAVILION, HANNOVER EXPO, 2000 — *ZERO*

ZERO — SPATIAL CITY BY YONA FRIEDMAN, 1958 — *ZERO*

ZERO — WALKING CITY BY ARCHIGRAM, 1964 — *ZERO*

ZERO — <u>L'ECLISSE</u> DIRECTED BY MICHELANGELO ANTONIONI, 1962 — *ZERO*

ZERO — <u>THX 1138</u> WRITTEN AND DIRECTED BY GEORGE LUCAS, 1971 — *ZERO*

ZERO — <u>ROME OPEN CITY</u> DIRECTED BY ROBERTO ROSSELLINI, 1945 — *ZERO*

ZERO — <u>2001: A SPACE ODYSSEY</u> DIRECTED BY STANLEY KUBRICK, 1968 — *ZERO*

ZERO — <u>THINGS TO COME</u> DIRECTED BY WILLIAM CAMERON MENZIES, 1936 — *ZERO*

ZERO — <u>TRON</u> DIRECTED BY STEVEN LISBERGER, 1982 — *ZERO*

ZERO — ROME AS SEEN IN <u>BELLY OF AN ARCHITECT</u> DIRECTED BY PETER GREENAWAY, 1987 — *ZERO*

ZERO — <u>PLAYTIME</u> DIRECTED BY JACQUES TATI, 1967 — *ZERO*

ZERO — LONDON AS SHOWN IN <u>28 DAYS LATER</u> DIRECTED BY DANNY BOYLE, 2002 — *ZERO*

ZERO — WORLDS OF IF, 1973 — ZERO

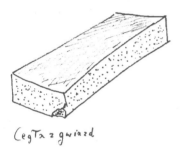

ZERO — BRICK FROM STARS BY STANISLAW LEM — ZERO

ZERO — SPACE SETTLEMENT: THE CALL OF THE HIGH FRONTIER BY PROFESSOR GERARD K. O'NEILL — ZERO

ZERO — THE COLONIZATION OF SPACE PHYSICS TODAY BY GERARD K. O'NEILL, 1974 — ZERO

ZERO — FUTURAMA AT NEW YORK'S WORLD FAIR, DESIGNED BY NORMAN BEL GEDDES, 1939–40 — ZERO

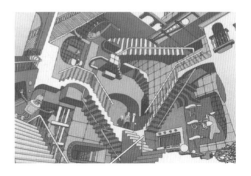

ZERO — FUTURAMA, CREATED BY MATT GROENING — ZERO

ZERO — SOVIET CITIES ON THE MOON? IN <u>SCIENCE DIGEST</u>, 1958 — *ZERO*

ZERO — EAGLE NEST – AN ARCHITECTURAL FANTASY BY JOSEPH HENRY WYTHE, 1948 — *ZERO*

ZERO — THE ATOMIC BOMBARDMENT OF NEW YORK (AND ITS AFTERMATH) PAINTINGS BY CHESLEY BONESTELL — *ZERO*

ZERO — LAIKA, THE FIRST LIVING CREATURE FROM EARTH TO ENTER ORBIT — *ZERO*

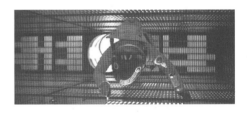

ZERO — HAL 9000, CENTRAL CORE, 2001: A SPACE ODYSSEY — *ZERO*

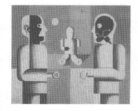

ZERO — <u>BRAVE NEW WORLD</u> BY ALDOUS HUXLEY — *ZERO*

ZERO — THE SOLAIRE REFLECTOR AT ODEILLO — *ZERO*

ZERO — <u>SUPREMATIST COMPOSITION: WHITE ON WHITE</u> BY KAZIMIR MALEVICH, 1918, MOMA, NEW YORK — *ZERO*

ZERO — <u>ABYSS</u> BY DRISS OUADAHI, 2006 — *ZERO*

ZERO — <u>DEVICE TO ROOT OUT EVIL</u> BY DENNIS OPPENHEIM, 1997 — *ZERO*

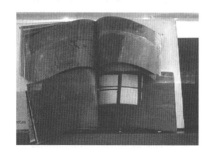

ZERO — <u>BOOK EDITION</u> BY GORDON MATTA-CLARK, WALLPAPER, BUFFALO PRESS, 1973 — *ZERO*

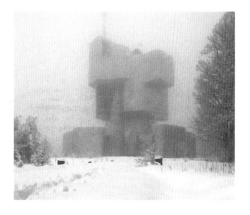

ZERO — <u>SCENE FOR NEW HERITAGE II</u> BY DAVID MALJKOVIC 2006 — *ZERO*

ZERO — <u>DWELLING</u> BY CHARLES SIMONDS, 1978 — *ZERO*

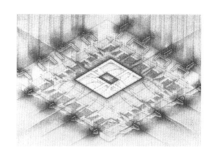

ZERO — <u>THE OPAQUE CIVILIZATION</u> BY WILL INSLEY — *ZERO*

ZERO — <u>GHOST PARKING LOT</u> BY JAMES WINES/SITE, 1978 — *ZERO*

ZERO — <u>CONICAL INTERSECT</u>, 1975. 27–29, RUE BEAUBOURG, PARIS. COURTESY OF DAVID ZWIRNER, NY AND THE ESTATE OF GORDON MATTA-CLARK — *ZERO*

ZERO — <u>COLOUR READING AND CONTEXTURE</u> BY JACOB DAHLGREN, MALMÖ KONSTHALL, 2005 — *ZERO*

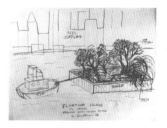

ZERO — <u>TRANSFORMATION</u> 'ERZWAGGON' BY HANS HOLLEIN, 1963, SAMMLUNG DES MUSEUM OF MODERN ART, NEW YORK — *ZERO*

ZERO — <u>FLOATING ISLAND</u> BY ROBERT SMITHSON — *ZERO*

ZERO — <u>SCIFI WAHABI NR 1</u> BY JOHN POWERS — *ZERO*

ZERO — <u>BUS HOME</u> BY DENNIS OPPENHEIM, 2002, BUENAVENTURA, CALIFORNIA — *ZERO*

ZERO — <u>FLORAL FONT</u> (DETAIL) BY CHARLES SIMONDS, 1989 — *ZERO*

ZERO — <u>THE LIGHTNING FIELD</u> BY WALTER DE MARIA, 1977 — *ZERO*

ZERO — PARK AVENUE BY GLORIA GAYNOR, 1973
— *ZERO*

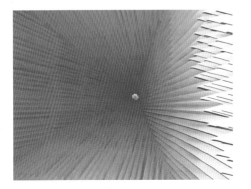

ZERO — ANECHOIC CHAMBER — *ZERO*

ZERO — THE KILLING FIELDS BY MIKE OLDFIELD, 1984
— *ZERO*

ZERO — MORTON FELDMAN, 1926–1987 — *ZERO*

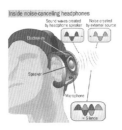

ZERO — BOSE NOISE-CANCELLING HEADPHONES
— *ZERO*

ZERO — LRAD; LONG RANG ACOUSTIC DEVICE — *ZERO*

ZERO — GOING FOR THE ONE BY YES, 1977 — *ZERO*

ZERO — SILENCE BY JOHN CAGE, 1961 — *ZERO*

ZERO — SECOND LIFE CREATED BY LINDEN LABORATORIES — *ZERO*

ZERO — SHIRLEYSHOR.COM/MEDIA/SHIRLEY/XANADU. JPG — *ZERO*

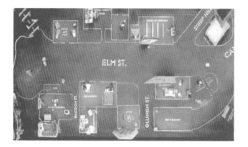

ZERO — <u>DOGVILLE</u> DIRECTED BY LARS VON TRIER, 2003 — *ZERO*

ZERO — SIMCITY GAME BY MAXIS (FIRST DESIGNED BY WILL WRIGHT, 1989) — *ZERO*

ZERO — GRAND THEFT AUTO: VICE CITY STORIES, 2006 — *ZERO*

ZERO — ATTENDA, GRID, EBOY — *ZERO*

ZERO — MANHATTAN IN THE 1930S, <u>KING KONG</u> DIRECTED BY PETER JACKSON, 2005 — *ZERO*

ZERO — VR-HELM — *ZERO*

ZERO — SAN FRANCISCO FROM FLICKR.COM — ZERO

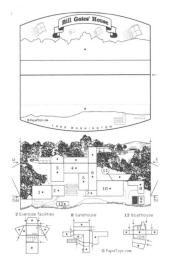

ZERO — BILL GATES' HOUSE BY PAPER TOYS.COM — ZERO

Chrysler Building

ZERO — CHRYSLER BUILDING ON 42ND STREET AND LEXINGTON AVENUE BY PAPER TOYS.COM — ZERO

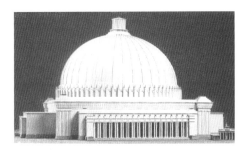

ZERO — ALBERT SPEER'S MODEL FOR A NEW CAPITOL BUILDING FOR A NEW NAZI BERLIN — ZERO

ZERO — PLARAIL FROM FFFOUND.COM — ZERO

ZERO — BLUE MOON CITY – BOARDGAME — ZERO

ZERO — COBOLHACKER.COM – MOVING HOUSE ON WHEELS — ZERO

Back to the

House of the Future

IPRO 301

Spring 2006

ZERO — EMERGENCY HOUSING BY SHIGERU BAN — ZERO

ZERO — ADD, IPRO 301 — ZERO

ZERO — DENKMAL 3 BY JAN DE COCK, KERSTIN ENGHOLM GALLERY, SCHLEIFMÜHLGASSE 3, VIENNA, 2003 — ZERO

ZERO — FREEDOMSHIP.COM— ZERO

ZERO — INFLATABLE CHURCH.COM — ZERO

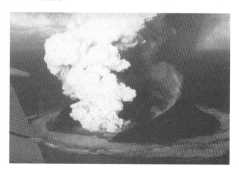

ZERO — SURTSEY ISLAND ON 30 NOV 1963, 16 DAYS AFTER ERUPTION — ZERO

ZERO — <u>URBAN RENEWAL #6</u> BY BY EDWARD BURTYNSKY, APARTMENT COMPLEX, JIANGJUNAO, HONG KONG, 2004 — *ZERO*

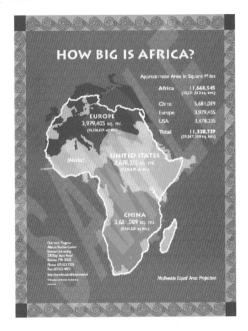

ZERO — WWW.GENERATIONALDYNAMICS.COM — *ZERO*

ZERO — <u>ALEPPO</u> BY LOTTIE DAVIES, SYRIA — *ZERO*

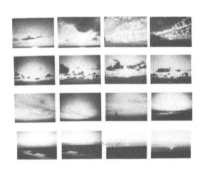

ZERO — ATLAS PROJECT BY GERHARD RICHTER — *ZERO*

ZERO — SEASCAPE SERIES BY HIROSHI SUGIMOTO — *ZERO*

ZERO — NANPU BRIDGE INTERCHANGE, SHANGHAI, BY EDWARD BURTYNSKY, 2004 — *ZERO*

ZERO — HONG KONG CENTRAL — *ZERO*

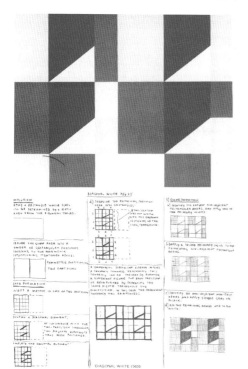

ZERO — <u>PALM SPRINGS</u> BY CHRIS BROWN, NEWTON, US — *ZERO*

ZERO — FFFOUND.COM — *ZERO*

ZERO — RIYADH, SAUDI ARABIA FROM ASTER SATELLITE — *ZERO*

ZERO — CHOCOLATE BROADWAY — *ZERO*

ZERO — <u>TOWNSCAPE</u> BY GORDON CULLEN — *ZERO*

ZERO — BARCELONA, 1992: PARALYMPIC CHAMPION ARCHER ANTONIO REBOLLO SHOOTS THE FLAME TO THE ALTAR — *ZERO*

ZERO — THE PRESIDENTS OF IRAN AND VENEZUELA LAUNCHED CONSTRUCTION OF A JOINT PETROCHEMICAL PLANT — *ZERO*

ZERO — IN LINE WITH GOOD CHINESE TRADITIONS, THE STONE IN THE PICTURE WILL BE BURIED UNDER THE BUILDING'S FOUNDATIONS — *ZERO*

ZERO — LAUNCH OF TITANIC, 31 MAY, 1911 — *ZERO*

ZERO — STALIN, VOROSHILOV AND KIROV AT THE OFFICIAL OPENING OF THE CANAL — *ZERO*

ZERO — CEREMONIAL SCISSORS.COM — *ZERO*

ZERO — MÖVENPICK HOTEL AMSTERDAM CITY CENTRE — *ZERO*

ZERO — 4 JULY 1828, RAIL CONSTRUCTION — *ZERO*

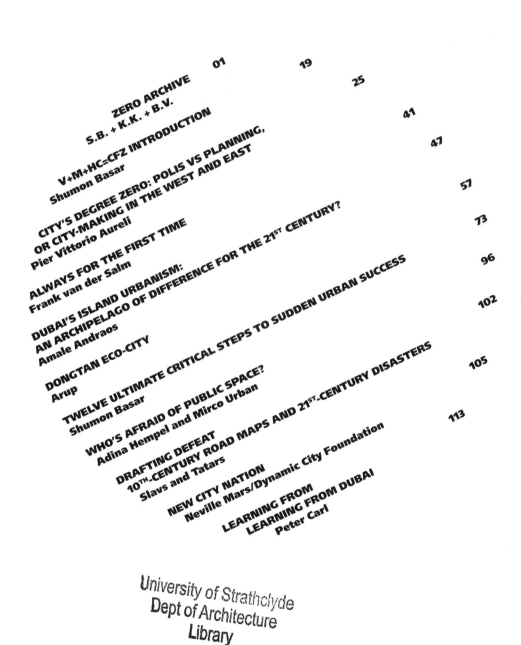

V+M+HC=CfZ/ Introduction
Shumon Basar

<u>Vision plus Money plus Historical Circumstance equals 'Cities from Zero'</u>. Rising precociously from desert, sea and redundant rural settings, Cities from Zero are unapologetic expressions of new-found economic — and therefore political — prowess in the 21st century.

The authors in this collection, which grew out of the Cities from Zero symposium held at the Architectural Association in London in November 2006, share a particular focus on the Gulf Emirate of Dubai and the rapid urbanisation of China. Organised by the Social, Urban and Political Cluster, the symposium brought together architects, critics, urbanists and documenters to ask: are these new urban experients universal blueprints for a better world, or doomed, out-dated models of already extinct ideologies? Or, even, something else entirely?

Someone recently told me about the first genetically produced lab chicken; they also claimed that provenance-free poultry will put to rest — once and for all — the ancient and perplexing question, 'What came first, the chicken or the egg?' Humankind has always been obsessed with origins: When did time start? Where did we come from? How did the universe begin?

Billboard at Hong Kong Airport, August 2007
(*Photo: Shumon Basar*)

19

The further back you go in history, the more you find that facts are inseparable from mythology. No one is really sure when the first city came into existence, but many different civilisations mythologise the first city as theirs. For a minute, though,

Next to Dubai Marina's Manhattan-esque skyscraper forest is a private beach and verdant lawns (*Photo: Shumon Basar*)

forget the past. What about the history of the present? Or, as Jean Baudrillard proposed, the history of the future?

It's been hard to ignore a recurrent statistic favoured in newspaper articles and architecture biennials which tells us that for the first time in history over 50 per cent of the world's population now lives in cities. And that figure will rise. Dramatically. Maybe irreversibly.

We may not know what the first-ever city was, but we now know that 'city' is humanity's terminal destination.

As George Bush and his government quietly retract the use of the ex-neologism 'axis of evil', a new 'axis of power' is emerging in the 21st century, one that threatens America's status as lone super-power. Economists have forecast that within decades China and India will become the first- and second-largest economies in the world. Today, in late 2007, China is already number two. This gives some reason to believe that its ascent to the top may occur even sooner than predicted.

Post 9/11, billions of dollars of Middle Eastern investment have been diverted from the United States back into more local interests. This is one of the major factors contributing to Dubai's extraordinary boom in the last few years. The 'Dubai-effect' — where massive amounts of liquid capital is turned almost instantly into high-value concrete property — has given rise to the second largest building site in the world, only superseded by China in its sheer maniacal consumption of steel. Neville Mars points out in 'New City Nation' that in 2001 the Chinese government announced plans to build 400 new cities by 2020. During the same period, Dubai made strident claims to host 15 million tourists per year by 2010, a number that is ten times its current population.

These may seem like the hubristic ramblings of autocratic regimes whose PR people are just a few doors down from the state propaganda offices. But the evidence so far indicates that these non-democracies have developed virulent forms of state-controlled capitalism that turn vision into actuality at remarkable speed.

New Beginning, Dubai (*Photo: Shumon Basar*)

Decision-makers in Dubai have no doubt studied China's successful strategy of Special Economic Zones in the 1990s — such as the city of Shenzhen. They have since deployed similar, only significantly more specialised tactics, as Amale Andraos points out in her text on 'islands' as experimental micro-planning.

An everyday shrine to the power of McDonalds and KFC, Guangzhou, China (*Photo: Shumon Basar*)

As a group, the authors of *Cities from Zero* contend that Cities from Zero are still, relative to the well-trodden analyses accorded to historical cities, the subjects of our collective ignorance. Or, worse still, they become the targets of lazy, supercilious presumptions and derision. Mike Davis and Daniel Bertrand Monk have coined the phrase 'evil paradises' to refer to new kinds of urbanisation fuelled by 'savage, fanatical capitalism'.[1] These critics unequivocally accuse Dubai of being 'the most remarkable and sinister' ring-leader in a gradual move towards 'new geographies of exclusion and landscapes of wealth'.

There is no doubt that demands for human rights to be upheld in all places — new and old — must be supported. However, the critic should also be fully aware of the 'where' that he or she speaks from. This 'where' is our culturally embodied position — it binds us with some, and distances us from others. The 'where' must always be taken into account during the act of criticism.

Pier Vittorio Aureli's exposition argues that the fundamental DNA of the European city is genealogically 'other' to the traditional principles of Chinese city planning. The physical attributes, in both cases, are the function of (a)political dimensions and the representation of power. Which is why, as Adina Hempel and Mirco Urban discuss, the liberals' desire for 'public space' in Dubai is a yearning for a spatial typology that has no proper political provenance in the region.

Alejandro Gutierrez, a director at Arup, and a driving force in the first 'Eco-City', Dongtan, near Shanghai, China, describes their urban vision as 'a process and not a product'. It's like burgeoning political agency: it rarely happens all at once. In the *lingua franca* of sustainability politics, the zero that is pushed for at Dongtan is probably that of 'zero emissions'.

Frank van der Salm's photographs are 'possible truths' about the stylistic iconographies found in Far Eastern Cities from Zero, how they repeat and differ. Even the future can induce *déjà-vu*, though many Chinese will tell you that it is the West which is hung up with the status of 'images' there, and that it matters little for the Chinese themselves.

Peter Carl reminds us that the City from Zero is in an almost folkloric pull between a techno-Utopian fantasy of delirious efficiency vs the tangible concerns of the human predicament. Aureli described this during the original Cities from Zero symposium as the city having to always 'decide about the undecidable'.

Etch-A-Sketch was a popular 1970s toy for children that allowed them to draw, erase, and redraw using straight lines only

'Zero-ness' recurs throughout history as a rhetorical and (thus) real paradigm promising the ever-new, like Nietzsche's Eternal Return. Every zero is located, particular. Simultaneously, the incessant and inevitable arrival of the 'next zero' renders all preceding zeroes quickly redundant. And redundancy is one of the risks of speaking about, analysing and depicting these global, urban debuts. By the time you read any of this, maybe all the places being discussed will have changed, moved on, mutated. To something better. Or worse. So why bother?

Because Cities from Zero are also effects and symptoms of a shared, supra-globalisation that implicates us all. We may be witnessing the future of our own modernities being played out vicariously elsewhere. Cities from Zero are visionary realms conditioned by special economic and political factors — that the West may find disturbing, incomprehensible and haunting — but that matters little to their proliferation and potency. Their very alien-ness may be an unwanted recognition of the West's inextricable role in their formation. And also, in their inextricable, mirror-image fates.

Now that the pesky problem of chicken/egg origin is solved, maybe we can turn science's brilliant minds towards the next unanswered mystery: what came first, the city or the dream?

1.   Mike Davis and Daniel Bertrand Monk, *Evil Paradises: Dreamlands of Neo-Liberalism*, London, Verso 2007, pp. ix-xvi

City's Degree Zero: Polis vs Planning, or City-making in the West and East
— *Pier Vittorio Aureli* —

Persistent whispered belief among the architectural community suggests that what makes a city is not its built form but the life and the relationships that take place within it. This belief posits that built form is always seen as something dead, soulless, completely devoid of any specificity that is not the arbitrary will of individuals — clients and architects — to impose a form of place on people who will inhabit that place. After the euphoria of the 1990s when everything that was solid seemed to have melted in the flows of globalisation, architects now feel guilty — or at least uncomfortable — when they face the built reality of a city. It is a reality clearly represented, framed and sometimes imposed through its architecture. Thus, architects find ethical redemption in an *a posteriori* conclusion that the inhabitation of the city always exceeds its physical limits, and so the form of the city cannot reveal anything essential about how it develops and acquires its 'real' social, cultural and political consistency. This mentality has been further nurtured by the fact that, due the political imposition of 'capitalist liberalism', the formation of cities is rendered as something fluid, informal, almost natural. It is as though it shares (with the same *non calanche*) qualities with which economic growth is characterised: a fluid, informal and natural ground for the evolution of humanity.

In this scenario the city seems devoid of any project, or any *a priori* mentality, of any form. It becomes a form only when it appears finally in the media-friendly photographs of Andreas Gursky, Thomas Struth and their countless imitators. The city as man-made object — the human thing *par excellence* as beautifully defined by Claude Levi-Strauss — is treated as a

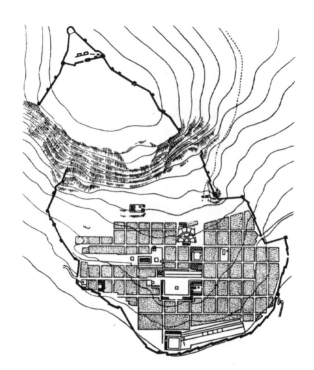

visual readymade, the backdrop for our value-free speculations on its 'content'.

I would like to counter this trend by presenting an opposing argument. It is that the very form of the city, as it is manifested through architecture and the places that it frames, reveals civilisation's deepest political, cultural and social understanding of human relationships. To argue in this direction involves stopping for a moment the constant updating of the city's countless complexities and contradictions, to rethink its basic political and formal foundations — its degree zero.

In the light of the questions arising from the theme of the 'Cities from Zero' symposium, I will go back to the notion of the city's primary purpose as conceived in two civilisations that have *systematically* designed their own cities. The emerging interstitial argument inbetween these notes is that much of the deep political and cultural problematic stemming from the newly designed urbanisation in the East is only partially the outcome of recent globalisation. The most tortuous political dilemmas — such as the role of public space and cultural legitimacy of urbanisation models — are still bound to the anthropological identity of the formal conception of city as applied by the Greco-Roman and Chinese civilisations. In the following pages I trace the West and the East's fundamental purpose for making cities, respectively, as *polis* and planning.[1] With '*polis*' I identify the will to form the city according to an idea of political organisation based on the act of composing irreducibly different parts (such as the realms of the public and the private). With 'planning', I identify the will to form the city according to a holistic scheme that goes beyond the separation of the public and private.

POLIS — In the *Grundrisse* Marx wonders whether the epic forms of Greek arts and culture make any sense within a civilisation based on industrial modernity, 'Is Achilles possible with powder and lead? Or the *Iliad* with the printing press, not to mention the printing machine?'[2] asks Marx. He realises that even if the original figures of Greek thought cannot be replicated literally in the modern age, their conceptual power resists the course of time and still persist in our imagination as constant reference. For Marx 'the difficulty lies not in understanding that the Greek arts and epic are bound up with certain forms of social development: the difficulty is that they still count as both norm and as an unattainable model.'[3] We can say that even in our own current modernity the Greek *polis* is still a challenging reference, if we assume that city is not only an infrastructure but contains politics in its very idea.

   As is well documented, *polis* is not the city as currently understood but is a state at the scale of a city. For this reason the formal organisation of the city has inspired the notion of politics — *not the other way around*. Politics concerns the question of how the inevitable conflict among individuals gathered in one place can be neither denied nor resolved but rather acknowledged and subjected to an imposed form. *Polis* — the city — *is* politics, and so the city is a political form *par excellence.* That is, it is the product of a decision that in turn begins to define its form. The name *'polis'* emphasises immediately that the city is not a random agglomeration of population and things, but is instead a precise composition of constitutive parts. Even before the origin of Greek *polis*, the origin of the city itself was not seen as an automatic urbanisation stemming from material causes such as population density and new technologies.

The earliest cities, as they appeared in Mesopotamia 7000 years ago, originated from the need to organise trade by minimising conflicts, or at least to bind them to certain agreements. In this sense the origin of the city — its degree zero — is the tribe's fear of conflict and thus the search for an alternative to it.[4] These agreements needed a form, a singular point in the territory. This point can be seen in the tribe's shrine. Early southern Mesopotamian cities developed from the form of the temples that served for the ritual centres of gathering among tribes as an alternative to conflict. Gathering, rituals and the trade organised around the temples were then the origin of the city: a sublimated form of the confrontation stemming from the possibility of conflict. And this origin is quintessentially political and formal at the same time. The political and the formal emerge as ritualistic uses of a specific architectural space recognised as middle ground between otherwise conflicting tribes and family clans. This middle ground is seen as sacred space and a reference point in the territory. In the course of time it is marked by the presence of monumental buildings. It is precisely because of this emergence that, from this moment on, public spaces were formed around what we recognise as monumental structures. They serve to mark singular enclosed spatial formations in order to symbolise their difference from the open territory.

We can argue that this model constitutes not only the very city of the zero of urban civilisation, but also the first form of gathering from the zero of political organisation. However, if in other civilisations this model evolved as populations gathered

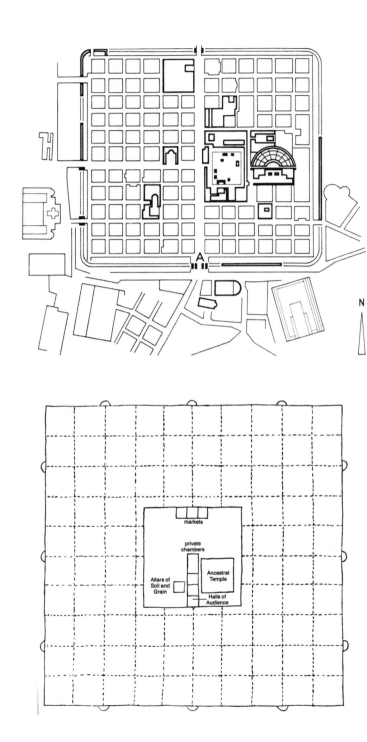

THE ROMAN CIVITAS. PLAN OF TIMGAD, ALGERIA. THE FORUM AS THE CORE OF THE CITY

N

markets

private chambers

Ancestral Temple

Altars of Soil and Grain

Halls of Audience

WANGCHENG, TYPICAL PLAN OF THE ANCIENT CHINESE CITY. THE RULER'S PALACE AS THE CENTRE OF THE CITY

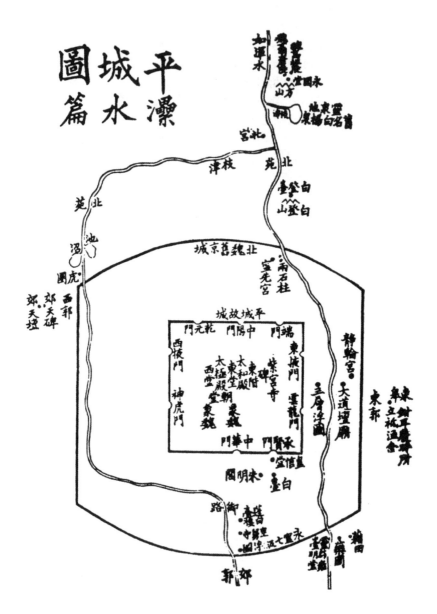

平城灅水篇圖

around the palace-enclave-temple of the king, it is in the *polis* that the king for the first time leaves his palace-enclave-temple in order to engage in *politics* — a confrontation with the many — in the space outside: the *agora*. With this defining act the Greek *polis* is immediately defined as a composition of two main forms: the *acropolis* and the *agora*.

Myths are nothing but the representation in form of an epic narrative of the encounter between chance and nature. In this sense the *acropolis* represents the very act of mediation between the natural condition and the human necessity of finding a defendable location for a community. Initially the *acropolis* is the citadel, the castle built on top of the hill. Like many cities predating Greek civilisation, it reflects the rigid monarchic structure of a community gathered around the defence structure of the monarch's palace. Gradually the monarch leaves his castle-palace in order to inhabit the space outside, and his enclave — *acropolis* — becomes a religious complex. The *acropolis* is gradually distilled into a mythical symbol: the beginning of the city. The city government exits this enclave. Once vacated by the ruler, his enclave becomes the *acropolis* and stands as the founding myth of the city — its *locus*.

In contrast to the *acropolis*, where the dominant factor in its form is the processional directionality of ceremony, is the *agora*, originally a marketplace. It is a rectangular space delimited by box-shaped buildings — the *stoà* — a form that emphasises their framing role by being open towards the *agora* and closed against the outside, the private world of the *oikia*, the private houses. If the *acropolis* represents the mythical origin, the *agora* is the very central political space of the community. The *acropolis* alone is still a citadel, a fortress; with the *agora* the original nucleus shifts from defensive necessity to the possibility of encounter and confrontation. The formation of the *agora* identified immediately a space that is neither the space of the ruler, nor the myth, nor the space of the private house.

Acropolis and *oikia* are what today we would call monofunctional places. The first is determined by religious identity, the second by family provenance. The *agora* by contrast is made of a composition of collective or semi-collective facilities that emphasise that its space is recognised by the many as *the* space for collective gathering. Its significance is further underlined by the fact that in the course of time it has developed from a marketplace to become a place for informal and formal discussion among the citizens. It is a place where the bottom challenges the top, by pressuring the ruler or through the deliberations in the assembly. The city is then a composition of tension between well-defined formal components, each defining a precise purpose of living together. The essential origin — the zero degree of the *polis* — is not a particular point, but the tension/relationship between its different parts. This tension/composition was formed originally by the contrast between the ceremonial form of the *acropolis* that represents the origin of the city and the framed space of the *agora* that represents the 'going outside' from that origin.

A similar tension is constitutive in the founding of Rome. Historians have tended not to give historical accountability to the legend of Remus and Romulus. Of these twin brothers, the latter is credited as the founder of the *urbe*. Recent archaeological discoveries have proved that the myth has a historical basis.[5] The myth of Romulus's murder of Remus (because he had trespassed the line traced by Romulus in order to indicate his own city, Roma) reflects the conflict among different tribes and their kings to gain political power over the archipelago of enclaves that formed the urban agglomeration prior to Rome. It is interesting to note that when Romulus took control of the confederation, after establishing his own city in one of the hills of the *Septimontium*, like the Greek ruler of the *acropolis* Romulus goes outside this limit to the valley below to open the *forum*, a gathering place for trade outside his own city. Indeed the word *forum* means *outside*.

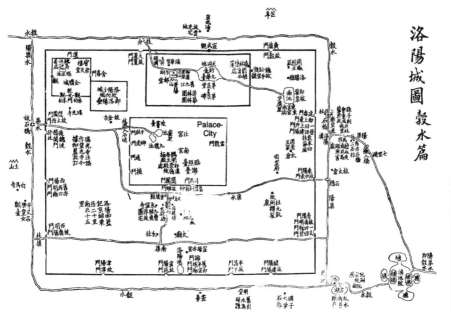

As in Athens, the foundation of the city as *polis* in Rome is not simply the building of the first nucleus around which to gather population. The foundation of the *polis* is the act of forming a communal space outside the tribe's enclave and so offering an open place where the many could freely gather. Even when the Greeks and Romans masterplanned colony-cities that included within them the *agora/forum*, this space always remain the true core of the city, not simply as the indigenous gathering place but also as the space of encounter between the indigenous and the visitor populations. Compared to other ancient civilisations the emergence of this outside space inside the city created the alter-ego of the *oikia*, the city intended as a gathering of houses. And it is precisely the sharp contrast between the composite public form of the *polis* and the introverted private form of *oikia* that was the origin of the contrast between politics and economics.

As defined by Aristotle, *technè politikè* is the governance of public space where people no longer acted as members of family clans but as individual subjects, while *technè oikonomikè* (from *oikos*, house) is the governance of the house where the role of each is strictly predetermined by parental hierarchies.[6] Cities in the West have over time evolved more and more

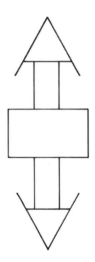

towards the hegemony of the *oikia* — the domestic space — over the *polis* — the public space. With the ascendance of absolute monarchy in Europe in the 16th century and the consequent formation of the power of the nation-state in the 17th century (with its bio-political apparatus of statistics and police-control immediately extolled by the rise of capitalism), cities have been shaped by the economy of their infrastructure. The accumulation of surplus seems to be considered more important than the political struggle of its inhabitants. However, the constituent urban and anthropological aspects exemplified in the Greco-Roman *polis* remain an irreducible prejudice in our way of looking and questioning the holistic planning of cities from zero such as those appearing in the Far East.

PLANNING — In the constitution of the Chinese city the act of planning has a different meaning than it has in the West. It does not consist of the abstraction of a scheme ideally projected upon a real situation. *Ex-novo* cities planned in a pre-modern China were conceived as the actual formation of a portion of territory according to the power hierarchies that human cohabitation entailed for them. The notion of 'ideal city' in China does not exist. The appearance of what we could call systematic city planning (based on orthogonal grids) began in China in the second millennium B.C. with the building of the early capital cities. Its form followed a basic type: a four-sided wall that enclosed a city gathered around another four-sided square that contained another inaccessible city: the ruler's palace.[7] This diagrammatic notion is the Chinese representation of the universe: everything must be inside, and what is left out is unknowable.[8] The efficiency of this pattern made China the place with the largest cities in the ancient world. Starting with the first contending dynasties such as the Shang and the Zhou, the capitals of the constantly belligerent states were often changing location.[9] Large populations were moved and relocated in a relatively short time unimaginable in the slower Western process of urbanisation.

It is therefore not entirely correct to assert that the speed of Chinese urbanisation results from her embrace of modernity (and capitalism) during the last decades. Since the very beginning of Chinese civilisation the culture of cities has been formed by the pattern of changing location almost as frequently as the transfer of power from one ruler to the next. Moreover, unlike the Greco-Roman cities where Athens and Rome always conceptually played an exemplary role, in early Chinese city planning there was no single authoritative urban realisation that could function as a unique reference.[10] China was immediately intensely urbanised by what today we would call 'instant cities' — cities that are highly consistent with a typological *modus operandi*, yet not referring to a unique model. During the feudal period a new ruler would rarely build up an inherited capital, but on the contrary would build his own capital on a new site. This production of cities was abnormally increased from the fifth to the third century B.C., yet all were born out of the same principle. This process of Chinese city planning is not at all comparable with the Greco-Roman system of planning cities. In the Greco-Roman world, Cities from Zero were meant to be permanent locations and indeed these sites became the basic structure for cities that survived the foundational political regime, which rarely happened in China. Another fundamental difference is that Greco-Roman foundation of cities consisted only in basic building — walls, roads and monumental buildings — while in China city planning entailed the building of the whole architecture of the city at once.

In the tradition of the Western Greco-Roman polis, even in its imperial period, the structures of power always had to confront other structures, making the city a composition of parts. In the Far East the whole city is designed and constructed as one continuous artefact: as one house. In this sense the purpose of the Chinese city before and during Empire is an exact fit with the diagram of the centralised power governing it. From a Western perspective, however, the most striking feature of the ancient Chinese city is the lack of public space.

If, in the Greco-Roman polis the core of the city is always an empty space — the agora/forum, in the ancient Chinese city the core is the emperor's palace, which, as distinct from the accessible agora/forum, is not simply enclosed but is completely forbidden. The interior of the city is immediately planned and divided into sectors according to the axis of symmetry established by the emperor's palace. Each sector is divided by large axial streets and great walls and each block in each sector is walled as well. The entire city is formed by a system of walls which organises the interior. In the course of its evolution Chinese imperial planning changed dimensions and forms of cities, but never its basic principle of the ruler's palace, followed by the grid of residences and different sectors symmetrically organised, each element acutely defined by a perimeter wall. It is for this reason that the Chinese word 'Cheng' can be both translated as 'city' and 'wall'. Early symbolic references to the city are pictographs that represent the city as what today we would call a gated community: walls and gates.

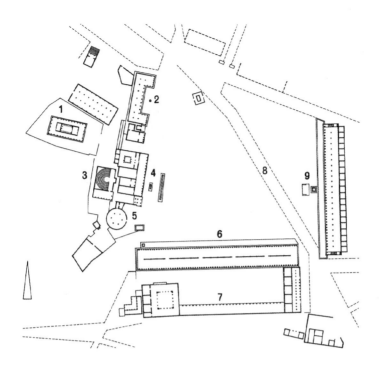

From a Western political point of view the Chinese imperial city is nothing but the *oikia* — the despotic logic of domestic space — extended to the whole of the city. Of course, the *polis* is also walled, and, as is well known, Roman cities were originally military camps. Passing through the Chinese city is nothing but the passage through walls: from one interior to the other. The city is conceived as an enclave and the fundamental aspect of its making is the establishment of boundaries. These boundaries are not the result of opposing elements as in the *polis*, but the outcome of the organic whole planned in advance by a centralised authority and shaped according to the rituals of the core, the ruler's palace. Greco-Roman mythology is peopled with tales of capricious gods, whose unpredictable attitudes helped the pluralistic spirit of the *polis* to emerge.

In China religion was immediately state-controlled and its manifestation personified and administrated directly by the rulers and then by the emperor. With the formation of the empire in 221 B.C. capital cities were more stable, but all new cities were built with the same principle addressing the central representative of the emperor. Modifications, deformations and transformations of the average Chinese imperial city would assert endlessly the structure of its basic principle to a point that all cities would appear (in the 17th century) to Giovanni Botero, as one continuous city.[11] Botero noticed to that this radical sameness made the cultural and social differences between city and countryside irrelevant and further, that the whole of China could be considered one continuous entity. The scale of the Great Wall itself, constructed at the beginning of the empire, appears to anticipate such a development.

Looking at contemporary Far East urbanisation from this historical perspective, one can hardly be impressed by the new development. The fact that new city building in China is proceeding at an unmatched pace can only be examined in tandem with a realisation of the underinvestment in what kinds of new city are needed. One has to realise that, in spite of the radical political changes that have take place in the last 60 years, and the economic turmoil of the last 20 years, China has developed and refined a city attitude consistent throughout the longest empire in world history. This mentality is clearly based on a conception of space that is not political — in the sense that we understand this term in the West — and of which the politics are control, fast implementation and ceremonial staging of centralised power. In this context of holistic planning, it is not surprising to hear statements on new Chinese cities such as this by the architect Qingyun Ma:

I would argue, perhaps controversially, that in China we do not need 'public space' as such because Chinese people do not need a space to be designated as such to be able to do public things. Even at the risk of sounding politically backward, I would suggest that we can put people together and find an agent that is intelligent enough to plan our cities scientifically, rather than be led by the aggregation of individual desires focused on acquiring and occupying bigger and bigger spaces, wider and wider ocean or park views and more and more happiness.[12]

RETURN TO DEGREE ZERO — Only by considering the irreducible, pragmatic differences of these two models can we avoid falling into unforgivable clichés in a consideration of the cultural and social transactions between West and East, especially when Western architects 'export' their urban expertise to the East. In the future the challenge of the City from Zero must be reinterpreted conceptually; in other words, not simply as what it means to produce new cities, but rather what it means to conceive new cities. What, conceptually speaking, is degree zero? And how does this degree zero unfold its form? I would argue that this zero degree contains the two fundamental conceptions of the relationship between public and private realms evidenced above. Of course, in contemporary urbanisation — both in the West and in the East — these two paradigms can no longer be seen in terms of a black-and-white duality. They are increasingly mixed (and the most extreme consequences of this mix can be seen in the high-tech feudalism of the new urbanisation of the Middle East). However I do believe that sometimes it's worth suspending the salutary inbetween attitude, and instead to look at things in a more dialectical manner. As Alexander Pope once said: 'If white and black blend, soften and unite a thousand ways, is there is no black nor white?'

1
I'm aware that is not entirely correct to consider the Roman City as *polis*. As is well known, the fundamental difference between the Greek and the Roman political systems is that the first was based on the autonomy of each city, in itself a state; the second was instead formed by a network of cities under the centralised power of Rome. Indeed in the case of the Roman city we should speak of *civitas* rather than *polis*. However in my explanation, which aims to extract urban paradigms, I maintain for the Roman city too the notion of *polis*. This is not only because Rome itself started as a *polis*, but also because the memory of the *polis* was at the roots of the Roman city evolution and identity of *civitas*.

2
Karl Marx, <u>Grundrisse: Foundation for the Critique of Political Economy</u>, Penguin, London 1977, p. 81.

3
Ibid.

4
See Michael Hudson, <u>From Sacred Enclave to Temple City</u> in Michael Hudson, Baruch Levive (editors) <u>Urbanization and Land Ownership in the Ancient Near East</u>, Peabody Museum, Cambridge Mass. 1999).

5
See Andrea Carandini, <u>Romolo e Remo. Dai rioni dei Quriti alla Città dei Romani</u>, Einaudi, Turin 2006.

6
Aristotle, <u>The Politics</u>, Penguin, London 1962.

7
In the 'kao gong ji' is the planning 'treatise' of Chinese capital cities. It was written around 500 B.C. and is the earliest book about capital city planning. According to its prescriptions which clearly reflect the trend of making the cities in ancient China, the city is a square of 9x9 Li (1 Li = 0.5 kilometre), three doors are on each side, there are 9x9 roads in the city, each road is wide for nine coaches, the ancestral hall is on the left, the temple is on the right, the Court or Boule is in front, the market is at the back, the palace is in the centre and all the other buildings should face it. See He Yeju, *Chinese Ancient City Planning History*, China Architecture and Building Press, Beijing 1996.

8
See Nancy Shatzman Steinhardt, <u>Chinese Imperial City Planning</u>, University of Hawaii Press, Honolulu 1990.

9
See Paul Wheatley, <u>The Pivot of the Four Quarter</u>, Edinburgh University Press, 1971.

10
K C Chang, <u>The Archeology of Ancient China</u>, Yale University Press, New Haven 1977, pp. 321–350

11
Giovanni Botero writes: '*My other reason is, for that it is not lawful for any of the Chinese to go out of their Country without leave or licence of the magistrates, so that, the number of persons continually increasing and abiding still at home, it is of necessity that the number of people do become inestimable, and of consequence the cities exceeding great, the towns infinite and that China itself should rather, in a matter, be but one body and but one city.*' Giovanni Botero, <u>The Magnificencie and Greatness of Cities</u>,
Theatrum Orbis Terrarum, Amsterdam 1979, p. 64. Interesting to note that Botero is one of the most important theorists of the absolute state in Europe, and the inventor of modern statistics as a scientific tool of governance.

12
As stated in the Urban Age Conference in Shanghai. See http://www.urban-age.net/10_cities/02_shanghai/shanghai_PL+US_quotes.html#Ma

FRANK VAN DER SALM

Bloom, 2006

Dynasty, 2007

'***Always for the first time***,' wrote Andre Breton, the emperor of Surrealism, in his paean to desire, *Mad Love* (1937). He was referring to love, and falling into it every time as though it was the first time. It's hard to deny the potency of this amnesiac principle. First times are full of fear and excitement. They come with innocence, and make the pioneer twinge with awkward prowess.

It's increasingly difficult to see anything 'for the first time' anymore. How many more images, places and people do we see today compared to someone 30 years ago, 60 years ago, 100 years ago? No doubt the answer ends with many zeroes, and it grows every minute. *Deja-vu* isn't some sensation felt only by the whimsically inclined. Familiar unfamiliarity is the very logic through which the 'new' propagates itself in our collective visual registers.

Frank van der Salm travels and takes photographs. Unsurprisingly, the photographer is drawn to places that announce their existence in the form of images on billboards, brochures and magazines. Cities from Zero are built in Photoshop first. The concrete and steel comes much later on.

The selection here is from Van der Salm's visits to the Far East. He always maintains that photography's relation to 'truth' is ontological and not mimetic.

Photography creates reality in the conditions of the image. When van der Salm photographs a place — such as the facade of a digitally animated tower or the neoclassical outline of a gated villa — he isn't necessarily interested in capturing the veracity of that place. Rather, he seems to want to show us how to look at that thing 'for the first time'. Sometimes this requires him to meld different negatives together — using the very same Photoshop that was used to generate the reality he records — to create an impossible view that manages to look probable.

Van der Salm has used the phrase, 'possible truths' to describe his work's relation to the real. Breton's falling in love 'always for the first time' again and again is like being addicted to the repetition of 'possible truths' each time around. So many images, so few truths. Never for the first time, except for the first time.

Text by Shumon Basar

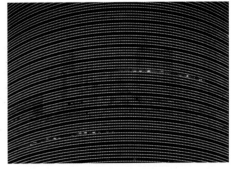

Mirage, 2006

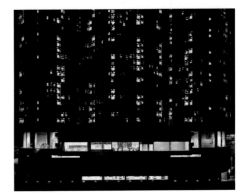

Gallery, 2004

Regime, 2005

FRANK VAN DER SALM

Link, 2004

Studio, 2006

Arcade, 2006

Dubai's Island Urbanism: An Archipelago of Difference for the 21st Century?

Amale Andraos

If there ever was a city from zero, then Dubai is it.

The concept of 'cities from zero' always seems to resonate with a certain nostalgia for Utopian projects: visions for better living in a brand new world and the possibility of abandoning everything to be reborn elsewhere — pure, absolute and out of nothing. It is the search for a *tabula rasa* — the ultimate ground for endless potential. Yet, on close examination, most of the Utopias that come to mind were never 'from zero' but entirely defined by what they were attempting to escape or reshape. Whether hovering above, floating next to, plugged into or removed from, the new cities these visions presented were almost always set in relation to an existing condition: that of the city — or cities — they were escaping to start anew. Whether one thinks of Constant's plans for New Babylon, Superstudio's collages of the Continuous Monument, Archigram's Plug-in City drawings or Kikutake's Marine City sketches, these new cities were always represented as an 'other' to the city they now rendered irrelevant. In contrast, Dubai's development in the last ten years is set with only the desert as its background and the overwhelming desire to transform itself into a city — 'a world-class city' — as its motor. This shift will make it the quintessential 'city from zero,' as aggressive a Utopian-developing effort as seen since the Romans — vastly different though their approaches are.

So what constitutes a 'city' according to Dubai? It is certainly not the locus of political expression, confrontation or representation. It is not founded on infrastructure, the Roman grid or the spinning out of a symbolic centre. It has no overwhelming sense of history — the physical embodiment of time — or even place, that could possibly be shaped by important natural geographical differences. Dubai's concept of 'city' is based on everything that has long been declared 'non-city'. Its morphological models seem to oscillate between Potemkin-like corridors of endless development along 'boulevards' (that are really highways) and the suburban model of cul-de-sac islands and private gated communities. Its political form is certainly not that of the *agora* or the *forum* and its ideal form is not that of the 'real' but that of the image. Dubai does not shape itself as the embodiment of an idea, rather its obsession with images of itself and of other cities dictates its making. Dubai is not a city formed by centuries of effort. Relative to other world cities, Dubai has formed in a matter of days.

Yet, at every turn, Dubai seems to distort these 'non-city' characteristics it adopts, inviting ever-so-slightly surprising possibilities and questioning the critiques too immediately expressed to dismiss it as a future new city — a 'City from Zero'.

EMIRATES HILLS, DUBAI SEEN FROM ABOVE (PHOTO: PETER CHAN SHU-KEI, CALAJAVA@FLICKR)

To illustrate how Dubai is emerging as a possible new model, one still needs to look — with an intentional dose of optimism — at its potential rather than its changing reality. And the best object of study to reveal these potentials is Dubai's fundamental unit of literal and symbolic development: 'the island' — a private and bounded mini 'city' or 'village' where all necessary amenities (living, eating, working, shopping) are provided, each island packaged with a distinct theme and style.

DUBAI'S ISLANDS: ICONS AND TOOLS OF DEVELOPMENT

While bounded (and themed) developments are certainly not a 'Dubai invention' — stemming from a long tradition that can be traced all the way from walled cities to Florida's Seaside — it is the young Emirate's adoption of the archipelago model as a conceptual, legislative and planning system of development that constitutes the uniqueness of Dubai's mode of creation as a city — a 'city of cities'. For these islands are not dispersed suburban havens — removed yet still connected to a centre, which they either still need or have supplanted. These islands are all equal centres, self-contained nodes appearing adjacent to one another and connected to each other by the thinnest possible road network. Parallelling its adoption of the skyscraper as architectural symbol of its embrace of modernity, it is the island — both literally and conceptually – that Dubai has embraced as symbol of its urban future – with the 'Palm Islands' as urban icons representing and announcing Dubai's debut to the world stage.

CONTROL ISLAND

At first glance, there are of course immediate issues with this 'island system'. While Roman cities were also islands along a road, their form was a grid – an open system that allowed endless expansion horizontally as well as infinite layering vertically — often of very different local expression (after all, no city or culture has ever complained of its Roman past). Similarly, one can compare 19th-century American gridded cities — now widely accepted as 'real cities' allowing for endless freedom of movement and by extension the possibility of civic life and participation — with the 20th-century proliferation of the suburban island model of development, endlessly stretching along highways and where public spaces of meeting and mixing have been relegated to the private spaces of asphalt parking lots and interior malls.

Dubai is the most fervent patron of this problematic suburban/island model that is prevalent today. Certainly Dubai finds these imported models of urban privatisation and development can be

THE REPRESENTATION WILL MELD WITH THE REAL (*PHOTO: AMALE ANDRAOS*)

conveniently adapted and easily adopted by the Emirate's highly controlling regime and mode of governance.

DENSITY ISLAND

And yet there are fundamental differences between Dubai's islands and their typological referent — the suburban development. The first difference is that of density, if not-yet real in terms of actual population, at least as projected by its buildings and organisation. When one thinks of the suburban 'island' model, one thinks of endless curvy rows of individual houses set side by side and neatly separated with well-trimmed lawns. While Dubai adopts this island model — where each island is called a 'city' with an adjective differentiating it from the next (Media City, Internet City, International City, Culture City) — it often combines it with intense density and heterogeneity, two characteristics always missing from the typical suburban model. Whether adopted by the vertical skyline of the Marina Towers, by the horizontal, tightly packed-prawn planning of the Palm Islands or even by the new-old artificial layers of Downtown Burj Dubai, the density at which all of these developments are conceived and then built emerges as a complete undermining of the image they attempt to convey as well as the model they are built upon — that of copious space and privacy for everyone: luxury for the masses. Dictated by the necessities of development for profit, the resulting density — if ever inhabited — could become a generator of the unexpected and the unplanned, a very real city which, while posing typical congestion issues, will also offer the potential to go beyond the glittery two-dimensional Walt Disney projected images of itself.

ISLAND AS CULTURAL BRIDGE

Second, to reduce the island model as a solely imported — mostly American — model of development conveniently adopted for its possibilities of control is to ignore the long tradition of expanded interiority and walled spaces that one can trace throughout Arabic and Islamic architecture and urbanism. From the typical Arab house with its courtyard and degrees of privacy to the different form of mixed-use 'complexes' that exist within Arab and Islamic history — from caravanserais along the Silk Road to palaces such as the Alhambra and to the later *kulliyes* — entire closed 'compounds' inserted within the existing fabric of Istanbul — the notion of a private enclosed space as a model of living and of development is very much a part of Muslim tradition, working well with its codes of being and living. And so the adoption of the island model could be seen as enabling Dubai to adopt certain aspects of modernity

INTENSE HOTSPOTS OF DEVELOPMENT (*PHOTO: AMALE ANDRAOS*)

while still maintaining its very strict Islamic adherence. In its application to rule its population and dictate its behaviour, Dubai's Wahabism is clearly different from that of neighbouring Saudi Arabia. Certainly Dubai's managing of its Islamic nature, together with its adoption of modernity, could open up possibilities for shifts in codes of conduct which in time will inevitably influence its neighbours.

PRIVATELY PUBLIC ISLAND

As a result, there seems to be a strange inversion of what we in the West consider the freedoms associated with public and private spaces. Whereas privatisation of public spaces is always considered to be accompanied by a reduction in civil liberties and freedom of expression, privatisation in Dubai — whether in the forms of the stretched interior spaces of shopping-malls or the interior of the gated community/island — actually brings forth an expanded code of behaviour. One can consider the veil or *hijab* as a means for a woman to extend her private space within the public realm, enabling her to move everywhere while feeling protected and respected by the covering. Within the confines of spaces owned by respectable Emirati families and corporations where gates, guards and camera surveillance are seen, ironically, to extend private and therefore permissible space where a woman can move unveiled.

Similarly, alcohol consumption in Dubai can only take place behind closed walls and within private spaces, and this can be seen especially in the city's resort hotels, bringing together Muslims and non-Muslims, locals and expatriates in unlikely proximity and mixing rarely experienced otherwise in conservative Islamic

WALLED ENCLAVES: RITZ LOOKING UP TO MARINA TOWERS

countries. And while it may be true that this model of private gated space — the island — might simply be giving the illusion of increased mobility as it works together with traditional Muslim codes of control, it is irrefutable that it also opens up possibilities for subversion.

EXPERIMENTAL ISLAND

The island model also promises the potential of 'micro-planning' — a skill Dubai has developed to implement its visions without relying on the heavy infrastructure and time usually required to implement comprehensive masterplans. Thinking of itself one island at a time, Dubai is able to test ideas, experiment and learn fast at small rather than large scales at any given moment in time. This has the potential to allow it to reassess and reorient its direction with the speed of a streamlined enterprise. After focusing on technology to attract business, Dubai moved to 'living' to attract families; then came shopping, entertainment and now culture, health and even 'green lifestyles'. Although it is easy to dismiss all of these as simply theming strategies and as sound-bite substitutes for public space and meaningful programming, it is not difficult to imagine the potential of such an approach. Given a slightly altered and enlarged focus, this multiplication of difference could become an incredible urban and architectural laboratory of ideas about urban life and especially about a smarter symbiosis with the environment, turning gated systems into real closed and self-sustaining systems, for example.

MODEL FOR THE 21st-CENTURY ISLAND
Then there is the refreshing embrace of ideas, of sheer will, ambition and vision. Whereas most of the already developed world seems stuck in nostalgia and suspicion towards the heroic and the visionary, Dubai's relentless competitiveness and willfulness offers at least the possibility of going beyond the known and the already imagined. Every island offers the chance to observe its precursors, learn and reinvent. And yet, it is this potential of the island system that is still very much unrealised. When it is not pursuing pure spectacle and modern prowess, Dubai shifts through the repertoires of 'themes' developing its own nostalgic styles everywhere — a 'new old'/Islamic postmodernism for pasts that have often never existed, a fusion of eclectic styles that resonate with a vague feeling of history. To go beyond surface transformation — limited to architectural and urban experimentations — and clearly develop difference and autonomy from one island to the next would require embracing ideas about different forms of living, about really mixing programmes and uses, about creating self-sustaining archipelagos where localised life is encouraged, multiplying local work, local schools and local shopping instead of multiplying highways and their unbearable traffic jams. What if Dubai's islands became an experiment for living to be exported back again to suburban models everywhere?

REAL ISLAND
Finally, there is the experience of place that inevitably always exists and is always different from its projected image. Dubai's photographs, renderings and billboards cannot convey the heat of its desert or the roughness of its building process and finishes. Similarly, its growing and changing population make-up — from hardened investors and business-class expatriates to more recent influx of middle-class 'refugees' fleeing nearby conflicts and choosing to invest in Dubai, intellectually and emotionally as 'home' — is shaping Dubai's reality away from its sound-bite

images. Inbetween the controlled and themed islands are emerging generic ones, each stretch with its own slightly different character, yet all more banal and more real — everyday places of living and working. There are the abandoned industrial areas with a few contemporary art galleries popping up. Even the labourers 'islands' — the infamous camps — are slowly surfacing to become visible, their voice struggling and yet inevitably growing louder in order to be heard.

If the 'island model' is replacing the Roman grid worldwide, then Dubai is the ideal candidate to study its potential and dream of its possibilities. While certainly a difficult enterprise, engaging it with the enthusiasm and willfulness that emanates from the young Emirate is certainly a more promising enterprise than sceptical fatalism. After all, even Rome was not built in a day. Dubai's first layers are only starting to appear and the moulding of its next ones is still far from known or understood, but the future may very well be just one archipelago away.

THE WEALTHY ARE ENTITLED TO THEIR PRIVATE LAND-LOCKED ISLANDS
(PHOTO: AMALE ANDRAOS)

For more information on Dongtan or Arup, please visit our website at www.arup.com

ARUP

DONGTAN ECO-CITY

PROJECT OVERVIEW

In August 2005 Arup was contracted by Shanghai Industrial Investment Corporation (SIIC) to design and masterplan the world's first eco-city, Dongtan, in Shanghai, China. In November 2005, we signed an additional contract with SIIC to work on three further eco-cities in China.

We are currently in the process of gaining final approval for the masterplan and design from the Chinese Government. SIIC will then invite international investors to take part in the first round of funding.

Dongtan will be a city of three villages that meet to form a city centre. The first phase of development aims to be completed by 2010, in time for the World Expo in Shanghai, and will accommodate a population of up to 10,000. The later phases will grow to a population of 80,000 by 2020 and are projected to rise with further development to a population of 500,000 by 2050.

The planning of Dongtan incorporates many traditional Chinese design features and combines with a sustainable approach to modern living, but not at the expense of creating a city that is recognisable as a 'Chinese' city.

For more information on Dongtan or Arup, please visit our website at www.arup.com

ARUP

KEY FACTS

• Construction of the city is due to begin in 2007.
• Some off-site infrastructure is currently being put in place by the Chinese Government; a bridge and tunnel linking Chongming Island with the Shanghai mainland.
• The Dongtan site is 86 square kilometres (8,600 hectares):
  — By 2010, the 1-square kilometre (100 hectares) first phase will be developed, to accommodate up to 10,000 people
  — By 2020, the 6.5-square kilometre (650 hectares) start-up area will be developed, to accommodate up to 80 000 people
  — In future development up to 2050, we hope to accommodate up to 500,000 people on around 30 square kilometres (3,000 hectares)

• The first phase to be developed will be the East Village which contains part of the marina and includes nearly a square kilometre of open space and parkland — we anticipate it will include around 2,500 to 3,000 dwellings.

ECOLOGICAL MANAGEMENT OF WETLANDS:

• The delicate nature of the Dongtan wetlands and the adjacent Ramsar site (www.ramsar.org) for migrating birds and wildlife, has been one of the driving factors of the city's design.

• We plan to enhance the existing wetlands by returning agricultural land to a wetland state to creating a 'buffer-zone' between the city and the mudflats — at its narrowest point, this 'buffer-zone' will be 3.5-kilometres wide.

ARUP

• Only around 40 per cent of the land area of the Dongtan site will be dedicated to urban areas and the city's design aims to prevent pollutants (light, sound, emissions and water discharges) reaching the adjacent wetland areas.

SUSTAINABILITY:

• To be truly sustainable, the city must not only be environmentally sustainable, but socially, economically and culturally sustainable, too.

• All housing will be within 7-minutes' walk of public transport and easy access to social infrastructure such as hospitals, schools and work.

• Although some may initially commute to Shanghai for work, there will be employment for the majority of people who live in Dongtan across all social and economic demographics – our hope is that within time and by effective policy incentives, companies will be attracted to Dongtan and people will choose to live and work in the city.

• Dongtan will produce sufficient electricity and heat for its own use, entirely from renewable sources. Within the city, there will be practically no emissions from vehicles – vehicles will be battery or fuel-cell powered.

• Farmland within the Dongtan site will use organic farming methods to grow food for the inhabitants of the city, where nutrients and soil conditioning will be used together with processed city waste.

• The development of techniques that increase the organic production of vegetable crops will

For more information on Dongtan or Arup, please visit our website at www.arup.com

ARUP

mean that no more farmland will be required than
is available within the boundaries of the site.

ENERGY:

• Energy demand in Dongtan will be substantially
lower than comparable conventional new cities.
• In buildings, this will be achieved by
specifying high thermal performance and using
energy-efficient equipment and mechanisms to
encourage building users to save energy.
• Transport energy demand will be reduced by
eliminating the need for a high proportion of
motorised journeys, and judicious choice of
energy-efficient vehicles.
• When it is completed, the energy used within
the city will not add to the level of greenhouse
gases in the atmosphere. Energy in the form of

electricity, heat and fuel will be provided entirely by renewable means.

• Energy supply will be via a local grid and with electricity and heat supplied from:

– a combined heat and power (CHP) plant that runs on biomass in the form of rice husks, which are the waste product of local rice mills.

– a wind farm.

– biogas extracted from the treatment of municipal solid waste and sewage.

– electricity will also be generated within buildings using photovoltaic cells and micro wind turbines.

• Some of the electricity generated will be used to charge the batteries of electrically powered vehicles or to produce hydrogen for

© Arup F0.13
Rev 9.2

For more information on Dongtan or Arup, please visit our website at www.arup.com

ARUP

vehicle fuel cells.

• A key feature of energy management in Dongtan will be the level of information provided to consumers to encourage them to conserve energy by means such as smart metering and financial incentives. A visitors' centre located close to the energy centre will explain how cities can be sustainable in energy terms.

RESOURCE AND WASTE MANAGEMENT:

• All waste in the city will be collected and segregated at source into at least three material streams.

• Waste is considered to be a resource and most of the city's waste will be recycled and organic waste will be used as biomass for energy production.

- There will be no landfill in the city and human sewage will be processed for energy recovery, irrigation and composting.

BUILDINGS:

- Where possible, labour and materials will be sourced locally to reduce transport and embodied energy costs associated with construction.
- A combination of traditional and innovative building technologies will reduce energy requirements of buildings by up to 70 per cent.
- Public transport with reduced air and noise pollution will enable buildings to be naturally ventilated, and in turn reduce the demand on energy.
- Buildings with green roofs will improve

For more information on Dongtan or Arup, please visit our website at www.arup.com

ARUP

insulation and water filtration and provide potential storage for irrigation or waste disposal.

• A compact city (made of three villages) reduces infrastructure costs as well as improving amenity and energy efficiency to public transport systems.

TRANSPORT:

• Dongtan will be a city linked by a combination of cycle-paths, pedestrian routes and varied modes of public transport, including buses and water taxis.

• Canals, lakes and marinas will permeate the city, providing a variety of recreation and transport opportunities.

• Public transport will use innovative

technologies, which may include solar-powered water taxis or hydrogen fuel-cell buses.
• Visitors will park their cars outside the city and use public transport within the city.

Last updated: 17 October 2007

For more information on Dongtan or Arup, please visit our website at www.arup.com

ARUP

Dongtan, East Village and East Lake (*Image by Arup*)

Dongtan, Harbour Flyover at Night (*Image by Arup*)

For more information on Dongtan or Arup, please visit our website at www.arup.com

SHUMON BASAR

TWELVE ULTIMATE
CRITICAL STEPS
TO SUDDEN URBAN SUCCESS

I'm fascinated by the phenomena of 'self-help'
culture. Visit any contemporary bookshop, and
you'll find a whole section devoted to titles
such as *Brand New Me, Fat is a Feminist Issue or*
The Power of Now. TV schedules are also crammed
with programmes that are aimed at saving people
from themselves and the barrage of ills that
plague those living in late-capitalist, liberal
democracies.[1] 'Self-help' culture seeks to empower
the individual subject by borrowing success
formulae from others. There's nothing truly
altruistic about this, though. 'Self-help' is a
billion-dollar industry that creates consumers
from weakened victims, and smiling, secular
preachers who offer swift salvation.
    I've come to take the success of 'self-help'
as a telling symptom of developed civilisations
that have attained a peculiar nirvana of liberal
contentment. As Jean-Paul Sartre pointed out, the
ultimate effect of true freedom is the tremendous
alienation of realising you're an existentially
free subject with no one or nothing to blame
your misery on anymore. Shopping, as many have
pointed out, has become one of the celebrated,
contemporary panaceas for market-driven, liberal
societies. Denuded of any vestige of religious
guilt (in other words, that materialism is evil,
greed is bad etc.), shopping is flaunted as both
harmless distraction for the unsettled soul (where
one more pair of shoes might make the magic number)

Dubai Properties Business Bay model gives an indication of the plethora
of uniqueness on offer (*Photo: Shumon Basar*)

At the Old Town development, by Emaar, the 'new' looks very 'old' (*Photo: Shumon Basar*)

and an economic bedrock for national and global markets to survive, and grow.

The logic of 'self-help' seems to operate at a much larger scale too. Countries may look at one another (or, sometimes, precisely *not* look) to dig themselves out of social or economic quagmires. Cities have begun to do this too. New York has confirmed that it's set to install a version of London's Congestion Charge control mechanism to cut down its own choking traffic problems. But we always expect famous metropolises to learn from each other. It's an exclusive club of urban like-mindedness.

Rarely do Western cities look to developing, emerging or 'third-world' cities for 'self-help'. Why would they? Progress, it is assumed, always migrates from the more developed to the less developed.

As we near the end of the first decade of the 21st century, resigned to the fact that humanity's future is in the future of the city, the fastest-growing urbanities are less likely to be in Europe than in the Middle and Far East. And by growth, I don't necessarily mean population only. I mean percentage growth in office space, in residential blocks, in infrastructure, in airport runways, in towers and bays and the anxious flux of semi-indentured, migrant labour.

For the last 15 years, the former British desert colony of Dubai has been an unstoppable site of unstoppable boom in tourism and business, fuelled by oil reserves that are now nearly dry and a global ambition bordering on hysterical hubris. The population has increased from 69,000 in 1969 to 1.5 million in 2007, which includes more than 200 nationalities living side-by-side. The city-state clearly follows the dictum that nobody remembers who comes second. Dubai is home to the world's largest marina, the biggest motorway intersection and will soon house the world's biggest shopping centre. At this rate, it will soon break the record for the location with most world-breaking records.

Shiny, new, over-scaled, scale-less, pompous, obscene, tasteless, but very real, Dubai is Utopian without ever using the word. It's visionary, but without the pesky obligation to be revolutionary.

Sure, part of me that feels that the 'Dubai mission' should be denounced as a bling-bland and deeply superficial vision, one that equates size with sexiness, like those 1980s macho-mobiles seen in *Magnum P.I.* or *Miami Vice*. Perhaps we should chide Dubai for forgetting (or, worse still,

A series of 200-meter-long illuminated and illustionistic billboards
presage re-enactments of history in the desert (*Photo: Shumon Basar*)

ignoring) lessons Western Europe could provide about the way in which a city's history must be layered over time, vertically, as though history were geology. If Dubai wanted to genuinely prove its liberal lifestyle leanings, it would begin to set a course in the honourable tradition of the European Enlightenment: lots of museums, libraries and other symbols of democratic representation. But is that the ultimate idea of the city for the 21st century?

If you stand on the main boulevard/highway, Sheikh Zayed Road — perhaps the best barometer there is for measuring Dubai's transformation from desert to downtown — all you see is an endless line-up of multi-coloured mirror glass skyscrapers: a city reflecting its own reflections, *ad infinitum*. Mirror glass is what architecture becomes when it wants to say something, but doesn't know what. Is there a more potent image of emptiness?

Yet there is a genuine attempt to construct the definition of a city-state in the 21st century which is fascinating to watch. Does Dubai simply press rewind? I don't think so. Unlike Berlin, which seems to long for a 19th-century past it actually once had but probably will never be able to recuperate, Dubai isn't hankering for a past it once lost — mainly because it never really had one to lose. It is desperately, defiantly and daringly looking for a destiny that draws images of the past, present and future into one jaw-dropping (and, for some, deeply disturbing) synthesis. There's no lamentation. No remorse.

So, if, for a moment, we look at Dubai as seriously as it looks at itself, might we discover tactics and strategies that signal new paradigms for cities in the 21st century — for other Cities from Zero. To put it another way: if Dubai were to write a best-selling, self-help book for other non-places desperate for a premium upgrade to the global stage, what might it suggest as the *Ultimate Critical Steps to Sudden Urban Success?*

1 /
BE GEOGRAPHICALLY REMOTE

A location stuck between scorched desert on one side and sea on the other may not sound ideal as a site to build a city on. But Dubai turns apparent deficiencies into positive assets. Advantage one of a *tabula rasa* that was traipsed over by Bedouin tribes 100 years ago is that there is no built history to contend with, no foundational

Already infamous, Nakheel's The World development is an archipelago of 300 man-made

forebears, no symbolic origins to tip-toe around.
Advantage two is that there is nothing to limit
growth. Like the fastest-growing city-sprawl in
the United States, Las Vegas, Dubai has virginal
space to expand into as and when it wants to.
So far, it plans to do so in both directions,
devouring desert and securing the sea.

2/
ALREADY POSSESS SIGNIFICANT WEALTH

Dubai struck oil in the 1960s, but even then knew
its supplies were relatively tiny next to those of

There are different geographies to traverse. Some are through time
and history, as in the China section of Ibn Battuta shopping mall
(*Photo: Nakheel*)

neighbouring Emirate Abu Dhabi. Dubai's gas and oil will last for 120 more years, but its oil is set to dry up by 2020. But who cares? By then it will have translated 50 years of oil-lubricated wealth into an ever-expanding portfolio of industries. According to the Director General of Economic Development in Dubai, 'When compared to $6.2 billion in 2000 and $4.4 billion for the year 1996, 2005's GDP of $13.6 billion puts the accumulated annual growth of Dubai's economy in the last decade at among the highest rate of growth in the world.'

3/
THE FUTURE CITY SHOULD BE ENVISIONED FROM ABOVE

In the Nakheel Showroom, tucked away behind high-security gates and set within flowing fountains and fauna, there is a meticulously Photoshopped aerial image of the Dubai that will take shape over the next 20 years. Sprouting off its coastline are three palm-shaped artificial islands, a crescent-shaped city for 750,000 people and an archipelago of islands known as The World. Inland, there is a 'city' planned in the shape of a falcon and another as a chessboard with 32 64-storey buildings for pieces. Everything is part of the big, planned picture. Sheikh Mohammed bin Rashid al-Maktoum, Dubai's Emir and visionary architect of change, is said to be a keen helicopter pilot. From his floating vantage point, the logic of Dubai's parts combines with a vision of the new city whole. This perspective — aloft, perpendicular to the quotidian ground — is an ancient, even celestial one for urban generation. Order once again comes from above.

'Sheikh Zayed Road's menagerie of different sameness'
(Photo: Shumon Basar)

4/
YOUR NATURAL CLIMATE IS NO BARRIER TO THE ECOLOGIES YOU CAN CREATE

In December, Dubai can average 29 degrees Celsius. By summer, it gets as hot as 45 degrees. Its average annual rainfall is just 30cm. But that's no reason not to have a rotating mountain that is snow-capped all year long or a waterworld with a 400-metre-long galleon ship, or an artificially cultivated green belt strung around an artificially dug river. It's the logic of air-conditioning and heating extended and amplified into a magic that can conjure up every ecology humans have ever coveted, and a few that have yet to be imagined.

5/
PEOPLE LOVE 'HISTORY'

There are three tenses in Dubai: new-new, new-old and old-new. When Bastikiya — an 'old' neighbourhood from the early 1900s with single-storey houses and courtyards — was being destroyed in the mid-1990s, someone evidently made the shrewd observation that 'Tourists like *old stuff*, so we need to keep some history. Let's rebuild Bastikiya!' And so they did. It may feel like it's just been removed from its shrinkwrap, but its narrow streets nevertheless invoke a more innocent time, countering the strident skyscraper-lust that pervades everywhere else. Next to the Burj Dubai, the slick 800-metre tower that is already the world's tallest building even during construction, is another development by the same company, Emaar Developments. 'Old Town' will be

medieval and castellated in its looks and boast
bubbling fountains and underground parking for
every resident. In other parts of Dubai, English
suburbia, American ranch-life and Arabian summer
palaces will all exist and provide copy-and-paste
memories. And 'The Lost City'(for fans of Indiana
Jones) will not be miraculously found but built
from scratch.

6/
A CITY SHOULD CONSIST OF MANY CITIES, VILLAGES AND WORLDS

Everything — from the smallest scrap of site
to the largest planned development is given an
ennobling name that evokes a village, a city, a
land or a world: KNOWLEDGE VILLAGE, DUBAILAND,
GIFTLAND, EASTLAND, HUMANITARIAN CITY, MARITIME
CITY, TEXTILE CITY, MEDIA CITY, INTERNET CITY,
HEALTH CARE CITY, INDUSTRIAL CITY, THE LOST CITY,
CITY OF GOLD, WATERWORLD, WORLD GOLD COUNCIL, THE
WORLD. Such appellations transcend locality and
nationality. Each '—Land' or '—World' is now the
summation of the idea by which it is prefixed, part
of a new and absolute index of place-identities.
From here, pedestrians and motorists traversing
Dubai become everyday travellers charting a
strange, scale-less geography.

7/
INVITE THE SUPER-RICH TO VISIT AND MOVE-IN FIRST

A room at the Burj Arab hotel costs $5000 per
night. Its 'seven star' status is just clever

PR hyperbole that was coined to convey its dedication to elite-luxury lifestyle. Each suite comes with its own butler, gold and chrome fittings are standard, and Michael Jackson drops in but doesn't stay over. David Beckham and his English football team-mates were said to be some of the first celebrities to buy in Dubai. Since then, Donald Trump, Versace and Giorgio Armani have decided to invest with their own branded hotels. Tax exemptions, perfect weather, golf courses, a doting and endless service class and a ruling class that exemplifies ostentatious wealth make Dubai the new gated attraction for the world's most visibly affluent. There's nothing filthy about being rich here. Monaco should be very scared.

Construction workers are ferried from building site to labour camp every eight hours or so (*Photo: Akis Pattihis*)

8 /
ARCHITECTURE MUST BE SKIN DEEP (AND THAT'S NOT SUPERFICIAL THINKING)

At Dubai Marinas, 200 towers have been built. Each one was cast in concrete. The collective effect during construction (especially at night) was of a coven of dark figures conspiring to attack. But their dull, atonal physiques were soon transformed. In Dubai, architectural individuality comes in cladding options. Applied like make-up for buildings, cladding comes flat-packed and is stuck on to the concrete. Bronzed steel, aqua blue glazing or pink granite finish? Instant differentiation! What's better still is that when the building is sold to a new owner, the cladding can be peeled off and replaced with a newer pattern. The Modernist rubric claimed the outside should be a function of the inside; Dubai, however, declares that the two have nothing in common, that they can live parallel lives.

9 /
INSTALL AN ALTERNATIVE TO PARTICIPATORY DEMOCRACY

Is it coincidence that the world's fastest-growing economies — China and Dubai — both eschew participatory democracies and espouse a hybrid form of state-controlled free-market capitalism? Both the Chinese Communist government and the United Arab Emirates' ruling tribal family believe the minds of the select few should map national visions for the many. Once decided upon, plans for

The Burj Dubai's superior height is set against Taipei's 101 Tower and the Petronas Towers of Kuala Lampur, an implication that Dubai is also an Asian city (*Photo: Shyman Bacon*)

the future are mobilised almost instantly into direct action. Any resistance to the vision goes unheard and is therefore useless. While cities like London and Rome are often held hostage by their history and those who insist on preserving it, Dubai encounters no such resistance to its grandiloquent strokes. Accountability comes only in the form of guaranteeing a lifestyle good enough for everyone to sacrifice their electoral representation.

10 /
DESIGNATE CONTROLLED ZONES
OF EXCEPTIONAL LIBERALISM

At its heart, Dubai is an autocratic Islamic state that closely monitors its media and its citizens. If this were its primary public face, it would hardly make for the best place in which to bask on the beach in a bikini or to run Reuters' Middle East operations. One of the first signs of legislative fine-tuning came when Dubai allowed non-nationals temporary citizenship in order to buy certain new properties. From then, more 'Freezones' were set up as legal lacunae excepted from the Emirate's primary social, economic and media orders. In Media City, now home to BBC, Al Jazeera and CNN, there is no interference from the Dubai authorities in any of the transmissions. At Internet City, you can surf through any areas of the web you wish, a privilege not granted to the rest of Dubai's residents. And the hotels that line the coast merrily serve alcohol to the skimpily dressed designer-clad crowd, where the chances of encountering an Eastern European prostitute are considerably higher than anywhere else. For those that take their freedom for granted, Dubai ensures that freedom is easily available.

11 /
IMPORT AN ENDLESS SUPPLY OF LABOURERS AND SERVICE CLASS FROM ABROAD

Some 400,000 labourers are building Dubai every day of every year. Most originate from Pakistan, India or Bangladesh, though now, the source countries are diversifying to avoid the build-up of an ethnic majority where there are only really minorities. In addition to the construction workers, recognisable by their blue jumpsuits, hundreds of thousands of other immigrants will and do form the service foundation for the expanding hospitality and finance industries. Labourers live in the forlornly named 'Labour Camps' of Al Quoz and Sunapur, gated ghettoes unmarked on any of the grand plans of Dubai. Non-unionised, bereft of any representational recourse to workers' rights, and housed in questionable living conditions, the throng that is building Dubai is in a semi-voluntary state of economic-human subjugation. Already the subject of scores of newspaper articles over the world, the plight of the migrant worker has begun to win a number of small, critical victories. Bad PR is like the plague for Dubai. In fact, 'Labour City' is already planned, proving that nothing in Dubai is unthinkable as thematisation or spectacle. Call it all an abject system of modern slavery, and those who work within it will tell you that here, at least, they earn money that would be unthinkable in their homelands. Such relativism is also the ultimate argument put by those shepherding this globally mobile workforce.

Dubailand will be by far the largest themepark in the world,
bringing together dinosaurs, space-ships, pirates and arctic zones
Photo: Shumon Basar)

12/
REBUILD THE WORLD –
ONLY BETTER THAN IT EVER WAS

'Our World is not a political world,' explains one
of the representatives from Nakheel, the company
responsible for laying out 300 man-made islands in
the shape of the world map. Countries and states
are on sale, at prices ranging from $6m to $40m,
for which you get a lump of sand and permission to
start your own micro-nation. Elsewhere in Dubai,
plans are afoot for a 1:1 scale Eiffel Tower,
the Pyramids of Giza, and a perennially wintry

snowdome. It's going to be the world's Best Of, a Greatest Hits of cherished geographies and icons. By rebuilding the world, Dubai hopes to sieve away the danger, the dirt and the dross. It wants to start over again. It's like *Pimp My World*.

To repeat: there's no lamentation, no remorse. Maybe that's the troubling thing for many academics and critics from Western Europe.[2] Dubai's guiltless and shameless thrust forward is not weighed down by an adherence to anyone's past. Where we in the West see huge postmodern quotation marks around everything that happens there, Dubai sees none. It sees the authentic production of the 'new', only bigger, and better, than anywhere else.

Perhaps the doom-mongers are wrong, and Dubai isn't a freakish one-off, but the very first of very many 21st-century Cities from Zero. And my guess is that the self-help guide is going to be a veritable blockbuster.

‒   1.

An indicative and impossible paradoxical example of this societal anxiety is the spectre of body-image crisis. On the one hand, magazines tell us that morbid obesity is on the rise, therefore we should eat less. At the same time, the media bellows about the pernicious dangers of 'size zero' aspiration that the fashion world 'forces' upon young girls — so beware of not eating enough. The 'too fat/too thin' crisis also exists for cities: codified in the diagnoses of 'super-cities' that are 'obese' with too many people and too few resources; and 'shrinking cities', that have atrophied under post-industrial failure or post-Socialist disarray.

‒   2.

See my essay, 'The Story of the Story', in *Bidoun*, Issue 11, summer 2007, where I explore the idea that the West's denunciation of places like Dubai and China must be seen in light of the West's waning economic dominance in the century that is now unfolding.

ADINA HEMPEL AND MIRCO URBAN

Numerous recent reports — whether in daily newspapers, specialist magazines or in mainstream TV shows/documentaries — have taken as theme the emerging city of Dubai, raising serious questions. It would be hard to avoid the impression that we in the West can no longer ignore the growing importance of the Arab world and, moreover, the shifting focus of the Western world towards the East. As diverse as these approaches might be — ranging from cultural and socio-economical studies, general introductions and reports from expatriates to critical surveys of urban and architectural phenomena — they reveal how our understanding of place, of culture, of cities, and of public space is changing and how we in the Western world are also changing.

Identity seems to be a major concern in contemporary debates. In the age of globalisation the urge to define clearly the identity of an object — as distinguishable from others and unique in itself — is the biggest criterion whether an object is classified as successful or just another ordinary piece. In case of a city, it's a bit more complex. Overarching elements such as the physical environment, the socio-cultural and economic context, the natural landscape, urban structure, aesthetic appearance and political power create (in the best case scenario) a rather electric and eclectic mixture, giving the city a more or less specific character.

WHO'S AFRAID OF PUBLIC SPACE?

How can we create identity?
How can we build a regional style without ignoring globalisation?
How can we develop a vocabulary that enables us to distinguish urban over-populated places in the 21st century from one another?

IDENTITY IN PUBLIC SPACE

One thing that we've learned is that the identity of a city lies often in its public space and in acknowledging its degree of control. According to Kant, 'public space is a place for public use of reason in opposition to private use of reason.' In other words, public space is where people can meet and gather openly and actively live the choices city life offers. Clearly there is a differentiation between public spaces as unplanned encounter and the public space above described as place for assembly or political action. The latter is connected directly to the state of democracy; therefore any debate about public space is also a debate about democracy and vice versa. Public space in this sense is an institutionalised space that demands a certain degree of order and control. These spaces embody the power of the institution. In a place like Dubai, where democracy does not exist as political system, public space in that sense does not exist. Any criticism about Dubai's lack of public space in the traditional sense as a place of deliberation is undoubtedly ill-informed and misplaced.

It is in Western society, where democracy seems to be a faded illusion or at least the ideology of democracy is stronger than its actual practise, that public space has existed — if only in informal parts of the city, where there is minimal control and surveillance — for the longest period. We choose not to engage in the discourses that declare the city is dead because there is no public space left; in fact, the changing degree and nature of publicness of such spaces is prefiguring the changing degree of the political environment and the state of our cities.

In Dubai discourses of publicness and debates about hiding the forces of control mechanism are simply unnecessary. Those places that are open to the public — such as Satwa Park or Creek Park — demonstrate relentlessly their degree of control, by monitoring crowds through use of gates and security staff. Dubai holds no secrets about its degree of surveillance — its open display of security mechanisms is something that adds to its appeal and the feeling of comfort in Dubai. We doubt that anyone in Dubai would claim to feel insecure, whereas in New York or London where people are under constant, more covert surveillance, fear is a big concern.

WHO'S AFRAID OF PUBLIC SPACE?

How can we call a place that is over-regulated — not only by architecture — public space?
How can we define central market spaces or train stations as public space just because
they are open to the public? How do we deal with security measures such as illumination,
enclosure and surveillance?

THE POWER LANDSCAPE

Much of what is built in Dubai is part of a wider plan, which is beyond human scale. The main protagonists of the city are local Arabs, members of the Al Bu Falasa family. We call them architects even though they have no academic education. They are shaping the environment in their own right. It is the desire of every architect to build and to give meaning to places through the act of building. The process of development from pencil lines to concrete walls gives pleasure and confidence.

Usually architects understand the process of building as a contribution to the city (and therefore to society) and to its identity. They believe that through developing their subjective ideas, they guarantee a better future for the location or/and an area (acknowledging that the act of design is a rigorously personal and emotional act). This process of building ideas and visions is flanked by that of enhancing power and highlighting a certain degree of independence.

Architecture always has been a tool embodying whatever power and resources a political institution might have. Dubai could be called a political power-landscape, consisting of built typologies such as the skyscraper, shopping mall and gated community, which display clearly the state of power politically as well as financially and technically. The Emirate Dubai is a highly planned and regulated landscape, where activities are regulated and organised.

WHO'S AFRAID OF PUBLIC SPACE?

Does it really matter if a design that is being built is authentic?
Does it really matter whether a building is spectacular or banal or original or 'fake'?
Does it really matter whether there is an existing masterplan or just a visionary idea?

THE IMAGE IDENTITY OF DUBAI

In a discussion about identity and power we also need to look at the imagery of Dubai. The fact that Dubai is looked at as a place that began its growth with the opening of the Burj al Arab back in 1999 shows how little many of us know and how much we miss out on. The already existing architecture in Dubai, whether in images or in reality, drew attention to an otherwise barely noticed place and, we would claim, an otherwise ignored swathe of land.

From childhood, humans collect images constantly, which give us the possibility to define the nature of an object. In the case of Dubai, assuming that most of us have not seen such a place before, other than in science fiction, we lack images to help us in this process. The image of a city full of skyscrapers, gated communities and shopping malls (typologies common in the Western world) in the desert is without doubt free of any antecedents. In fact it is Dubai-as-image that is now being sold to neighbouring countries.

Taking a closer look at the existing buildings, one could argue that the image of a design — the architectural drawing — holds more realism and graphic virtuosity in Dubai than the physical building, leaving almost no space for interpretation or curiosity. The representation is itself turning into an object — one is bound more closely to the reality of the image than to the reality of the actual built project. In this way, architecture becomes a tool in the power-landscape of Dubai; less important is how a building is realised aesthetically.

The desert has long been mythologised, at least in the West as a landscape of fear, one that is constantly changing and permanently present in the rendering of Dubai, adding to its image. The emptiness of the desert offers space for deceleration from the city. Architecture is necessarily connected to artificiality: any project or architectural vision is a projection on to the site. Even the most modest, most traditional building appears artificial and strange in the desert.

Dubai's identity does not rest in big architectural moments; in any case, much of what is being built is without the hand of the so-called 'starchitect'. Identity is not something that can be constructed through building or implementing visionary ideas, it simply grows from what is done and the way spaces are used. It is a rather complex phenomenon that must always be considered in the context of its time. With the city as a cycle of ever-changing entities and outcomes, there is no final identity nor is there a finished city.

WHO'S AFRAID OF PUBLIC SPACE?

What do the transmitted images tell us about the identity of a city?
What do we learn about the self-confidence in this radical change in dealing with history?
What can we learn through the growing Western criticism on the re-presentation of 'their' landmarks in the Arab occident?

THE IDENTITY OF CRACKS

Again and again, traces of the desert seep through the soaring skyline. In the organised and programmed landscape of Dubai there ought to be spaces that are left behind and stay beyond the influence of the so-called architect. At these sites the shift of scale from 'beyond-bigness' to human is conspicuous. Here, where the degree of power and control is deemed to be zero, the city can be truly experienced at its richest. Here, at least, we can be observers of how spaces that show more openness in terms of design or even those free of 'architecture', develop their own qualities. They offer space for activities for which no other place exists. At the border of the 'city' — without any specific need or programme — they turn into specific places through the way people use them. Their identity changes along with the activity.

These places, considered professionally as cracks in the over-designed/regulated landscape are filled with energy and confidence. They bespeak an urgent desire for something beyond the themed environment in Dubai. We would like to introduce the word 'voidscape' for these places. They are voids that are full of potential and identity. These voidscapes denote delights, surprises and experiences of time people may have there. In that, they are truly unique. Whereas the dynamic of the city is slowed down by the very act of building, such spaces predict change and fluidity. Dubai has many voidscapes and we believe that the city's urban potential lies in these sites. It is these very places where social encounters can take place that can be defined as public space in Dubai. Those 'natural' landscapes that make up much of Dubai's identity imply that even untouched nature is not as untouched as we might think; they are more filled with programme than the rest of the supposed urban landscapes.

WHO'S AFRAID OF PUBLIC SPACE?

Does the desert as a constantly changing element not already constitute an identity?
Is the void not displaying identification through the freedoms with which the space can be used?
Isn't it already a very brave undertaking to build a city almost from zero?

WHO'S AFRAID OF PUBLIC SPACE?

Cities from Zero: infrastructure as first element to lay out the structure of a city.
Any architectural element, whether it be a fence or a lamppost or a street or signage, marks
the process of urbanisation and inhabiting space.

(All images copyright Adina Hempel and Mirco Urban)

DRAFTING DEFEAT
10th-Century Road Maps and 21st-Century Disasters by Slavs and Tatars

We have always had an aesthetic weakness for the merciless and brutal banality of bureaucracy. Little did we know that such a weakness would extend to the bureaucrats themselves. The following are reproductions of 10th-century maps by Al-Istakhri (aka Ibn Khordadbeh or Al Farsi) found in a 1933 Soviet edition of Nasser Khosrow's *Safarnameh*, or *Book of Travels*. Both Istakhri and Khosrow were Persian bureaucrats whose legacy was a paper trail of the very antithesis of administration: a regime of curiosity that attempted to describe and map out the Middle East as a coherent geographic and cultural region. Khosrow, an 11th-century Persian poet and philosopher, had led an uneventful life as a tax collector in present day Turkemenistan when one night, in his sleep, a voice told him to leave behind his life of worldly pleasures. Khosrow dropped his

1. Iraq

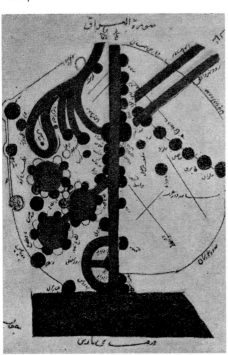

2. Syria

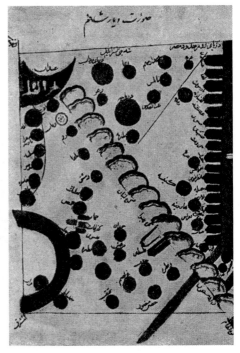

Maps by Abu Ishaq Ibrahim Ibn Muhammad Al-Farsi al-Istakhri aka Abu'l Qasim Ubaid'Allah Ibn Khordadbeh aka Al Farsi aka Istakhri

avowed weakness for the medieval Merlot and began immediately to plan a seven-year trip through the Caucases and the Caspian to the holy cities of Medina and Mecca. Khosrow was, to some extent, the millenary Muslim equivalent of a 21st-century born-again Christian. Except where the former asked questions, the latter offers only solutions. Where the former travelled extensively, the other is unlikely to have a passport.

Academia, the publisher of *Safarnameh*, was itself an unorthodox outfit in the Soviet landscape of the early 20th century with a reputation for smart, unexpected titles on relatively limited runs. These maps were drafted during a period when Islamic geography rekindled an interest in Roman and Greek scholarship abandoned by the Christian West. Early draftsmen including Istakhri contributed to *An Atlas of Islam*, with

3. The Caspian Sea

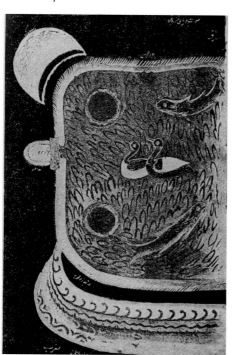

4. The Persian Gulf

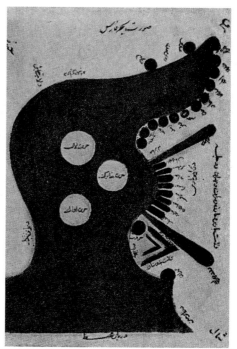

a visible bias for the Farsi-speaking peoples in the Middle East, where a boundless taste for geometric shapes and symmetry belongs today more to the world of fantasy than fact. Later cartographers such as Al-Idrisi went on to craft intricate maps on improbably luxurious materials (e.g. a 400-pound tablet of silver) with even more improbable names (such as *The Gardens of Humanity and the Amusement of the Soul*) that would

serve for centuries to follow. When Christopher Columbus studied these maps, before setting out to sea, we wonder: did it occur to him that his future would be no less unpredictable than our past?

5. The Arabian Peninsula

6. Egypt

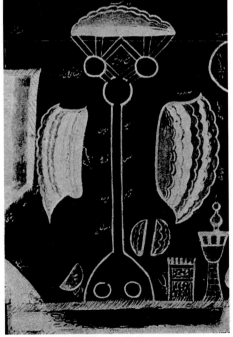

NEW CITY NATION
Neville Mars/Dynamic City Foundation

SHOCK AND AWE

In 2001 China's Minister for Civil Affairs, Doje Cering, formulated the ambition to build 400 new cities by the year 2020, a grandiose scheme that should accommodate the flood of rural migrants and elevate China to the level of a model industrialised nation. From the first moment I read this statement in a small article on the internet, the image of a continent built from scratch took hold of me. The obscene ambition to attempt to design an area on the scale of the European Union in less than two decades simultaneously shocked and mesmerised me. Three years into the project — and officially near completion — our research has only strengthened these two incompatible sensations of admiration and concern. Progress is made at a tantalising speed but it's mostly two steps forward, one step back. Often the solutions equal the problems. At the heart of this schizophrenic assessment lies the new city.

THE 400 FETISH

This project started with a simple fetish, at the time of the Iraq invasion in 2003. My fetish was for newness. Obviously this is not unusual — I assume this book is a product of the same fetish. For better or for worse, the world is shaped by people with this affliction, and architects seem to be hit particularly hard. A sinister urge to design everything in sight (to create newness) drives the profession. Urban design may be dead; the dream to shape man's greatest invention from scratch lingers on. The idea to design a complete urban system is highly seductive. If you could conceive a city from zero, its design would be free from all the accumulated problems, clutter and outdated infrastructure and outsmart the predicaments ageing cities struggle with. This is a powerful idea, especially when multiplied 400 times. It's an idea that has become one of the driving forces behind China's rapid renovation, engaging the entire nation from the policy-makers to the migrant sand diggers in a frenzied rush for progress.

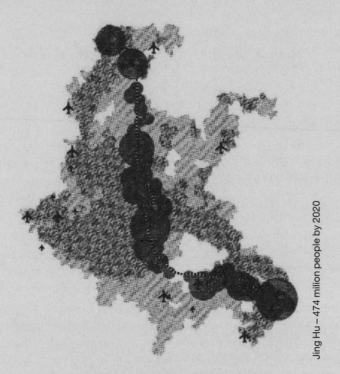

Jing Hu – 474 million people by 2020

MUD (MARKET-DRIVEN UNINTENTIONAL DEVELOPMENT)

In reality, for all but a few of China's cities, renovation means innovation. However, this is not necessarily a problem. New cities built on inspiration and idealism — like Brasilia and Chandigarh — have a bad track record. They are surviving today against the odds; their populations are reclaiming such precisely defined architectural spaces on their own, informal terms. Contemporary Cities from Zero are the result of much more lucid forces and are loosely assembled, more than designed. This could explain why many of them are much more successful. They adhere, at least for the time being, to the desires of a specific niche in the market. Manicured residential containers and meticulously themed retail parks cluster themselves around the highways. The aggregate cityscape expands producing unintentional forms. The city, like light, is ambivalent; neither planned nor organic.

The 400 Chinese cities to be built by 2020 will be the result of such an ambivalent process. This makes the birth of a city mostly a matter of politics. Depending on how you define a city — by population size, or maybe by its footprint — the official time of birth will differ. This is particularly true for Chinese cities. Detailed criteria are formulated which prescribe the ratio of urban to rural inhabitants in an area, and its ratio of rural to urban economic output. This may sound clear-cut, yet it results in cities at odds with our general understanding of a city. Finely dispersed semi-urbanised regions may obtain city status, while dense cores in the suburbs are overlooked.

STEADY PROGRESS

The current political climate in China is geared towards the creation of new cities but they cannot feature in the official statistics. Developers and migrants alike will need to be served, but not at the price of paying out more city-related benefits. This puts China's radical objective to build 400 new cities in perspective. During the period of 1978 to 1998 an unprecedented 23 new cities were realised on average each year; more than 400 in total. Today, by adapting regulations, barely one new city can officially be added each year. Yet the urbanisation process has never been faster and continues to accelerate. In built volume China is projected to expand the equivalent of a 25-country-large European Union within two decades.

At a time when, in the West, urban planning has become a painstaking and slow process, the Chinese boom seems to offer fresh opportunities to rethink the city. However, the absurdity of building 400 new cities in 20 years is not quite as stark as the aspiration to attempt their design. Any traditional notion of design will be inadequate when urbanisation occurs mainly at the two ends of the spectrum: bottom-up as doorstep urbanisation and top-down as an assembly of mega-projects.

The most distinct Cities from Zero are of the second category — built from scratch and at once. Although they do not comply with the official formulas, around 100 new towns of substantial size have mushroomed across China the last two decades in the form of mining and tourist towns, suburban enclaves, factory villages, themed and concept towns, military settlements. They emerge in

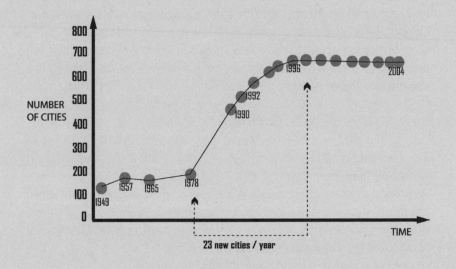

800
700
600
500
400
300
200
100
0

NUMBER OF CITIES

1949
1957
1965
1978
1990
1992
1996
2004

TIME

23 new cities / year

models of growth

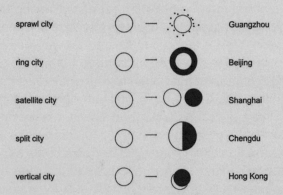

sprawl city		Guangzhou
ring city		Beijing
satellite city		Shanghai
split city		Chengdu
vertical city		Hong Kong

different forms, sometimes as independent entities, sometimes part of a larger urban structure, but always clearly delineated from the pre-existing. Medium-sized towns tend to favour the Split City model. Across the river or train-track on an empty plot of land the town is duplicated from scratch. Ignoring the old core, facilities and living quarters, a package design is implemented with minimum connections to the original infrastructure. The town reinvents itself and leaves its old form behind like a butterfly emerging from a chrysalis. Other models of rebirth include Vertical City (new looks down over old), Ring City (old is encircled by new), Sprawl City (new scatters and flees from old) and Satellite City.

The most recent wave of new towns is made up of residential satellites. Built in an instant, they are marketed actively and branded as new cities. All reference to the context or any previous condition is erased. Instead, historic features, whether Western ornaments or Chinese roofs, are often incorporated to promote the new-style living environment. They proclaim: We are not just new cities but 'Brand New Cities.'

ALL CITIES ARE NEW

This is an important distinction when in effect every town, city and metropolis in China is new. Even existing cities are regarded as *tabula rasae* waiting to be cleared. From the villages exploded to expand into a metropolis to the historic centres such as Xian, Chongqing and Beijing, which since the birth of the Republic in 1949 have seen a structural overhaul every single generation. The economic reform era introducing the final grand gesture has reshaped the capital beyond recognition. The fine texture of the *hutongs* (the rigid grid of communist work units that are the predominant spatial form in Beijing) have made way for an urban landscape defined by mega-icons and orbital arteries.

But this unilateral destruction of old built forms should be regarded within the context of a society that is in the process of inventing itself from scratch. The tradition of thinking of a city as a physical form is a limited measure for newness. The truly new city is inhabited by citizens who themselves thirst for newness. New buildings, as much as new products and fashions, are demanded by a generation of new consumers. The shifts in what is on offer can barely keep pace with the changing appetites of what will shortly become the world's largest and newest middle class. The mass migration of 450 million Chinese farmers is creating entire populations of first-time urbanites.

THE MEGALOPOLIS FROM ZERO

Though not as conspicuous as the Brand New Cities, the first category of bottom-up development has a much greater impact on China's new urban landscape. Although the new urbanites are flooding into existing cities, much of this migration is temporary. Policies installed to cool the hyper-expansion of existing urban centres create sprawling fringe developments with rolling populations. Counter-intuitively, the true impact of these migrants' urbanising potential is actually felt at village level. Remittances of urban capital facilitate the brickification of the rural environment, as does the return of workers with improved skills and knowledge. The combination of pooled home-grown investments and extensive rebuilding steadily encroaches upon once-rural land to form a loose-knit network of urban activities and forms. The pre-existing distribution of villages across China's eastern bulk was already at levels of density comparable with American suburbia. As each village starts to expand outwards, an almost contiguous tissue of development forms: an extensive splatter pattern of semi-urbanised inhabitations. The combined forces of expansion of the built environment, natural population growth, and the influx of an inter-provincial population will by 2020 coalesce to create a single enormous megalopolis stretching from Beijing to Shanghai. An area of 485,000 square kilometres of China will in effect become a continuous ridge city, with a population of 475 million distributed at a density of 978 people per square kilometre.

ZERO NEW CITIES

Growth, even in China, is not infinite. Many cities in the West are static, and several are shrinking. Looking at the numbers in China, it becomes clear that to accommodate the projected

450 million rural to urban migrants by the year 2020, in theory no new cities are needed. Growth can be restricted to the most efficient urban template: a well-defined network of urban cores of 2 to 6 million inhabitants. Suburbanisation, so often frowned upon, is transformed to efficient urban expansion with an influx of almost half a billion citizens.

Restricting expansion to the urban cores of the most efficient existing cities (those with populations of between 1 and 3 million), and doubling their populations would accommodate the migratory pressure. Rather than creating new cities, policies and clever planning can redirect the urban developmental thrust and contain it within current structures.

SUPER SATELLITES

While idealised projections can claim to solve the urban problem, the reality on the ground necessitates an integrated approach. It is crucial to unite China's two main forces of urbanisation, if any planning measure is to claim relevance. Satellites become unavoidable simply because they respond to the local need to develop. We have no choice but to try to conceive sustainable urban models applicable within China's market-driven high-speed context.

While we seek to discourage the creation of stark new cities, the development of satellites reintroduces the potential for large-scale design. Freshly legitimised, the designer is called back to the disintegrating developmental patterns and presented with a formidable task: to fashion a prototype that will produce healthy, attractive and spatially efficient new tissue around the existing mega-cities. Satellites though, even in China, have a notoriously poor track record. In the early 1950s the Beijing government planned 40 satellites to be distributed throughout the municipality. As the plan progressively failed to take shape, the number was reduced to 29, then 24, then 14. Today only three are deemed worthy of investment.

Satellites want to grow, compete and overtake, offering cheap space, land, facilities and labour. But they remain entirely dependent. The local metropolis is their *raison d'être*. They need to avoid the twin traps of being overly dependent on the mother city, thus falling to the level of a sleeping town, or too independent, risking on the one hand simple failure, and on the other becoming subsidiary nodes from which sprawl proliferates. Too close a positioning of under-designed satellites can lead to one expanding into the next, like cookies in an oven. Equally, satellites too far from the core offer diminished possibilities for public transport.

The failure of the designed satellite lies in its rigidity. Overly meticulous in its preconceptions, it is incapable of incorporating the flux of different users at one point in time, and different uses over a period of time. Static, sterile environments result which are doomed to economic decline. To avoid the reverse scenario presented by MUD — that of an almost blanket coverage of dispersed developments — the satellite needs to be planned, but also to acknowledge the legitimacy of market-forces as a morphological tool. The environment will need to be flexible to its users and capable of responding to their urges.

One key imperative for the successful satellite is critical mass. On this front China offers hope in that it has proved itself to be a context in which new development occurs on an enormous scale: neighbourhoods of 500,000, and satellites of more than 1 million people. At this level, the satellite in fact becomes the new town, the City from Zero.

Can satellites be designed to provide an efficient framework for market-driven development — in effect, to become super-satellites? You can try!

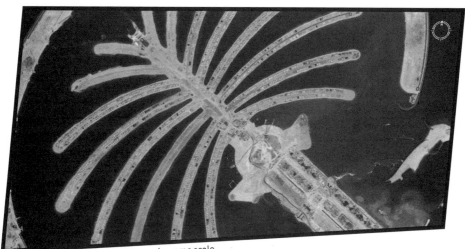

Dubai's Palm Island, above, shown at the same scale
as London, below

Learning from
Learning from Dubai
Peter Carl

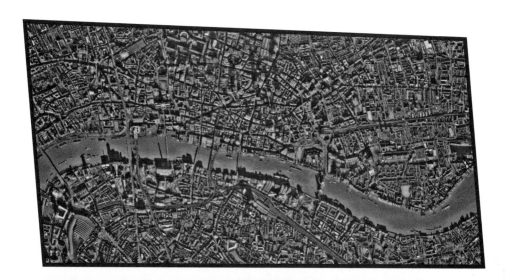

Completing the 144th floor of an undisclosed total, the Burj Dubai became the world's tallest building on 29 July 2007, and will continue to rise. Clad entirely in reflective glass, the world's tallest building will vanish into the sky. When completed, it will house 35,000 people, equivalent to half the total population in Dubai before the discovery of oil. The double-decker lift-cars hold 21 people (one of the decks must be able to carry one person more than the other). The air-conditioning, the Burj Dubai website announces, has a capacity equivalent to melting 10,000 tonnes of ice per day (perhaps literally, in Greenland). Fifteen million gallons of 'supplemental water' (condensation) sweat into the surrounding artificial lake each year. This lake, framed by the vast amount of housing and the huge mall which surround the tower, is depicted in the website's GTA-style video as a boating facility (with rather good digital wakes).

At the moment, the 50-mile view from the 144th floor to the south-west quadrant surveys a fairly sparse settlement, although the interactive Java map of Dubai indicates that this will eventually fill out with a roughly 60 per cent increase on the size of present Dubai. This future growth is centred on Dubai World Central, a composition of 750,000 people wrapped around the world's largest airport. And this airport is about half the area of the Dubai-land themepark, itself about the size of central Las Vegas. Indeed Las Vegas and Dubai grew up more or less in parallel; Sheikh Zayed Road is mostly office towers and hotels whilst the Strip is mostly casinos and hotels, perhaps confirming a fundamental similarity.

Commenting on the possibility that the Dubai property market might be levelling off, or 'maturing' (it is, at the lower end but demand for high-spec offices and residences, particularly villas, is still lively), Sana Kapadia, a research analyst on a recent report on Dubai's real estate market for EPG Hermes, responded to the interviewer from ArabianBusiness.com,[1] '... the construction will never end. Dubai will keep on building. Besides, things are not being built without a purpose ...'.

It is usually said that the purpose of all the fantastically pleasant, unsustainable evocations of a new global presence is the need for Dubai to find income after the oil runs out; and oil sets a high standard for income and for pleasantness. A more sublime, but representative, expression of this purpose is expressed by HH Sheikh Mohammed: 'We have to make history and approach the future with steady steps, not wait for the future to come to us.' (AME Info, 2 May 2006). The Sheikh's phrase, 'steady steps', understates a velocity that is more like the 40mph lifts in the Burj Dubai. It is impossible not to marvel at the sheer speed and scale by which Dubai has established itself not only as a paradigm for a 21st-century Islamic city, but possibly as a paradigm for 21st-century city-making in general. The Sheikh believes that 'history' can be made through the construction

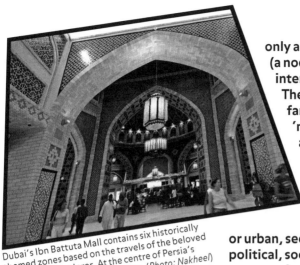

Dubai's Ibn Battuta Mall contains six historically themed zones based on the travels of the beloved 14th-century explorer. At the centre of Persia's grand dome is a Starbucks outlet. (*Photo: Nakheel*)

only a moment of intensity (a node) in global financial interconnectivity.

The metaphor evokes a familiar contest between 'market forces' and architecture, which has always been easier to win in the design of individual buildings than of cities. 'Growth', whether financial or urban, seems regularly to invoke political, social, environmental, ethical compromise. The principal design techniques for such cities as Dubai or Song Do (or the literally named King Abdullah Economic City, Saudi Arabia by Dubai developer Emaar) are rooted in the suburban mall, where crowds of consumers flow smoothly past reassuringly packaged exotica available for purchase. Even 30 years ago these malls – machines for maximising footfall, controlled environments blessed with good cheer, good behaviour, good health all set to music – had begun moving into cities and to develop the 'experience' that simulated 'real' cities. From here it is a short step to resort (themed) urbanism, culminating in Dubai's 'Internet City' and 'Media City'; and indeed 'all that is solid melts into air'.

MIRAGE URBANISM

Dubai is also the new Las Vegas in architectural theory. However, when Rem Koolhaas, in the useful *Al-Manakh*[2], advises us to learn from Dubai, he is not deluded into proclaiming the semiotics of 'popular

of a service-city, one that satisfies high-income desires and is executed architecturally as a double game between abstract form and historical reference (every historical style can be found distributed around Dubai, often combined). That is to say, postmodernism texture-maps applied to infrastructure. This belief is not restricted to Dubai. Prequelled in China, it can be found also, for example, in the rhetoric surrounding the development of Song Do Intelligent City, 'Gateway to Northeast Asia' (in other words, a rival to Hong Kong), which is attached to Incheon Airport and retailed as a Ubiquitous City (wireless comms everywhere) 'combining the best of Paris, Venice, Sydney and New York'.

This use of 'gateway' – by now a cliché of economic eschatology – deploys a primitive spatial metaphor to conjure a sense of earthly, rooted location where in fact there is culture' which animated *Learning from Las Vegas* (1972). He is fully aware that these cities require a platinum card for entry (along with a predilection for golf). Whole cities have become brands, products of the sophisticated titillation industry. Koolhaas bridles at Mike Davis's rendering of Dubai[3] as the collaboration of Speer and, even more offensive, Disney, less because Davis has overstated his case than, one suspects, because Koolhaas is worried. An important aspect of Koolhaas' reputation derives from his ability to render shopping with analytic wit at Harvard University, or to envision Prada stores as global performance epicentres, web-quakes (air and earth again) on screens hung off the shopping-rails.

It was a scandal to Western architecture schools when Michael Graves installed the Seven Dwarfs as caryatids on his Team Disney Building (1987, with Gruen Associates, descendents of Victor Gruen, author of the first enclosed mall), in fulfilment of Michael Eisner's search for 'entertainment architecture' that would make him smile. The arguments and designs of AMO/OMA have made it cool, perhaps necessary to ride the wave (for those with scruples, otherwise it is the mainstream). Presumably until some tasty interiors are completed, the Burj Dubai website (www.burjdubai.com) strives to evoke (offer for sale) the lifestyle of the building by harvesting the product ads found in architectural journals. These derive from the formula of design + art photography + lifestyle, first worked out in the Bauhaus.

So none of this is really new (and certainly has nothing to do with being Arab or Muslim). Moreover, even earlier, was 'culture' so much more intact when the world's fairs — proto-malls laid out as urban gardens, set in the future — were the authoritative embodiments of art + industry + commerce? Excepting masterpieces, has not capitalism always exercised this interdisciplinary effort to capture history with more exuberance than taste, more quantity than quality, more fantasy than wisdom? At least since World War II, have not the architecture students at world-class universities come mostly from suburban consumer-scapes, acquired the classics as the basis for design-ethics at university (somewhere between Socrates and revolution-through-form), and then brought up their children in the consumer-scapes they have meanwhile helped to amplify? Does not Dubai differ only in its imagery from Archigram's supposedly revolutionary shopping-rave in an oil rig?

Of course Marx's *aufhebung* of solid into air is correct, as are Benjamin's inability to make sense of arcade-culture and Baudrillard's more abstract rant against simulation: the milieu they describe is indeed *unheimlich*. But hey, this is what we are — bourgeois: caught between a vague moralism (from authenticity to family values) and a canny amoralism (profiteering and hip consumerism). There is no difference of class (including emirs and sheikhs), only of ability to pay. Accordingly, there is nothing to inhibit conceiving Dubai as a high-margin 'luxury' item. This 'nothing' is the zero of the proposition.

It is plain from the commentary in *Al-Manakh* that Koolhaas/AMO's potential endorsement of this position stops well short of proposing that the year-end shows at architecture schools begin to look like the annual Cityscape property trade fair held in Dubai.[4] Here the void of museum-space replicates the empty desert's assumed lust for architecture – whole cities are for sale. This three-day event brings out all the special effects: huge, luminous parametric phallus is bigger than that one, but the latter has more curves, or more iconography, like the collection in *Icon*'s June 2007 issue (048), curated by Foreign Office Architects). It is a bigness that seeks to attain a celestial halo of translucency, reflectivity, colour (always blue skies and water, lurid green grass and palms), photo-unrealism. Bigness sublimates itself into the techno-light that moves from AutoCad or Rhino screens to the HD plasma-screens where it is most at home (coining a new style – Plasma).

The Burj Dubai is the world's tallest building

models, animations and renderings ('visualisations'), forms restrained and warped, iconography usually kitsch, crippled architecture like that found in computer games, all accompanied by music, ornamental women, robots, deals, even complete contradiction: the face of Che Guevara over the slogan, 'Join the Property Revolution'. Bigness strives to be importance (this

Burj Dubai is supposedly based upon 'Islamic principles of design' (in fact, D'Arcy Thompson), whereby a white flower with three petals underlies the radial geometry that governs the ascent of the structure to an evanescent, reflective superiority of altitude (view). The push-button gratification afforded by the computer in all this 'air' is difficult to ignore

— the finger that pushes the 'render' key expects a response from the finger that enters a PIN number, which in turn triggers a 'build' key: power and pleasure delivered through iPhone urbanism.

TOWARDS ZERO

Having suggested that zero points to a possible moral vacuity, it is necessary to further clarify the concept of Cities from Zero. Dubai is built on the edge of the Arabian Desert, and it is tempting to think of this as better than brownfield, since lines can be drawn anywhere — even in the Gulf. The context is as apparently empty as a computer screen. It is obvious though that such topographies are not invented from scratch.

Dubai skims the foam off the most recent developments of the service city and its bourgeois lifestyle, floating in a global economy that required at least half a millennium of development (from the time of the Dutch East India Company and the European conquests in the Americas and the Pacific — these were economic, as opposed to the previous theo-political, empires). Moreover, this is possibly the most resource-intensive lifestyle imaginable (even before it is placed in a climate where 30 degrees Celsius is 'cool', accompanied by high humidity, two weeks of dust-storms, etc.); and, in that sense, its ecological dependency is vast, less than zero (except in oil, while it lasts— local natural gas presently drives the power and desalination plants).

Making and running Dubai depends upon the most sophisticated technology — global airline networks, high-speed data, construction methods, and so forth — and this too does not come 'from zero'. It is because of this technology that Dubai can be built so quickly; but, despite the tendency to think of technological achievement as progress and progress as history, the mere fact that there was a desert yesterday and a city tomorrow does not mean that 5000 years of urban history have been erased. If anything, Dubai and its lookalikes presume to create the zero on which their freedom is based.

There is indeed a question as to whether the term 'city' aptly describes such abstract machines. Technology has been applied throughout — Dubai comprises a narrowly defined (economically, not ethnically) body of residents whose needs are channelled efficiently through themed zones (the historic part of Dubai is being 'restored' to conform to the themed experience). There is nothing else. Only the (world's largest) container port seems to have escaped theming; even the immigrant workers' camps become *de facto* themed areas of a less-than-zero kind.

Compare Fatimid Cairo, for example, where a wealthy sheikh would build a palace and perhaps endow a mosque or school or hospital or bath, and these would be inserted into a pre-existing urban topography. The resulting conflict, negotiation, accommodation, collaboration exerted a profound claim upon individual freedom. Indeed the Koran presumes an urban context of this kind. It is tempting to say that, in Dubai, the sheikhs are trying to develop this context. However so much of what one expects to find in such a context is absent — perhaps even prohibited — from Dubai that one is forced to speculate in either of two directions. It could be that Dubai is intended to be a trickle-down city, meant to attract diversity as a supporting population, the way Calcutta was laid out as a foreground of nobles against a background of servants, or the way the European Union began as an economic agreement, whereas Charlemagne started with Latin.

Here we are to imagine the bourgeois finally overcoming their self-loathing, redeemed in a city of palaces and consuming, made credible through design. Alternatively, one must think at a much larger scale — the parts of a city distributed across a region, perhaps along the 400-mile coast of the UAE, or even larger. The missing context is disposed in the interstices between such nodes (for example, Dubai's neighbouring Emirate Sharjah?), or found in the interior of Africa or Iran or Iraq. Forget the concentric city — Istanbul and its infinite sprawl; think of a regional network, with urban nodes of different character (had the neocons in Washington not thought in terms of defeating — creating — 'evil' but had simply designated Baghdad an economic free-zone, Baghdad could have held supremacy in this network, at a profit rather than a devastating cost; and Halliburton would have

built a shiny Tower of Babel). The physical network, finally, is only an ecologically expensive fragment of the global economic network, a system of attractors for the proceeds derived from capitalising the world's peoples.

Both these alternatives allow Dubai the scope to pursue a freedom from the customary constraints of being human (including freedom from Sartre's other people), a freedom achieved through design technology. If, however, all is air and anything is possible, why the endless *nouveau-riche* office and hotel towers thrashing 'form' to discover another nuance of awe; why the need to bring along history (intimations of quality or simply a useful device for telling one zone from another?); why so unoriginal or, as the critics inevitably say, 'banal'? As projected, Dubai comprises about two-thirds the area of London, but with one-quarter the people. Architecturally and socially, it effectively converts this amount of London into Canary Wharf. Koolhaas may be worried because Dubai suggests that the more authentically 'global' ('world-class') a city is, the more it seems to valorise the least attractive aspects of bourgeois culture, and the role of design in securing them. Having declared New York 'delirious no more', Koolhaas is uncomfortable with the cloying sincerity by which so naive and vacuous an alternative is, literally, retailed.[5]

Mall-urbanism allows one to critique a city of this size. It is a flat, systematic order, lacking the ontological depth of traditional cities.

Only by converting the city into a project of design technology can one entertain the dream of a milieu purified of crime, disease, poverty, conflict, and sublimated into an air-conditioned visual spectacle. This summarises Le Corbusier's Ville Radieuse (1924), an attempt to achieve salvation through construction of a better world Marshall Berman famously saw as 'the experience of modernity' and traced it back to Goethe's *Faust II*.[6] Berman does not develop the long history of reification (Lukacs) or enframing (Heidegger) which underlies the phenomenon; but, however blinded by progress, one must acknowledge a regressive history, a history of producing less with more. Moreover, the air that Dubai colonises might be only a preparatory stage, if Ray Kurzweil is correct in his assumption that computer processing power equals quality of thought (a version of pro and contra in *Are We Spiritual Machines*, 2002), and that Moore's Law will bring on the convergence of genetics, nanotechnology

Le Corbusier's temple and car comparison updated: above, the church-mosque-museum of Holy Wisdom; below, Los Angeles computerised traffic management. (Sources: above, pictaloge for flickr.com; below, BLDGBLOG, 'The Geometry of Traffic Control', Wednesday 26 October 2005)

and robotics, resulting in a globally connected 'intelligent' entity (perfect and exhaustive memory, light-speed thinking, blah) for which humanity is merely the chrysalis. The evaporation of civilisation (and its resources) into self-replicating smart dust seems to me a return to zero – to the original biota from which we arose – and a confirmation of the hypothesis that techno-progress invokes historical regression.

ANYTHING TO LEARN
There are three possible readings of *Al-Manakh*'s declaration, that '[Dubai, or King Abdullah Economic City] is architecture's redefinition, whether it is welcome or not':[7]

a) The *unheimlich* simulation-scape is the new (= now, relevant) stage of 'history'. Its unruly spectacle drowns any fundamental difference between the most kitsch hotel and the work of Rem, Zaha or what *Al-Manakh* terms virtual unknowns (small offices – although to me, many of the gigantic firms are actual unknowns). Architecture, even cities, are 'product', more or less interestingly ornamented infrastructure, or mere ephemeral brands in the global orgy of consumption, or simply more or less attractive metaphors identifying a few gigabytes of economic information ... air rather than solid (but nonetheless deeply demanding of the planet). There is only good or bad design, forget pretensions to 'culture'.

b) This is in fact the way bourgeois capitalist architecture has always behaved (including the use of immigrant workers). Dubai is a legacy of the 500-year effort to transform the disorderly, less salubrious parts of the town (the renaissance Comic Set) into a supposedly nobler, more orderly, beautiful, healthy, efficient, profitable topography (the renaissance Tragic Set). The possible correlation between techno-aesthetic order and political or social order is trapped in bourgeois ethical ambiguities.

c) This game can still be won. There is still scope for substance, depth, meaning; but it calls for a significant reinterpretation, or reorientation.

It would seem that (a) is simply an extension of (b), and does not, in fact, represent anything new, perhaps even a regression. This suggests that current design generally is ill-prepared to make a new city. Largely, this is because ethical interpretation of both market forces and current technology is still an unresolved problem. If resource-depletion does not establish a true limit to global capitalism, the expectation will unfortunately endure that technology (the true character of modernist design) will eventually deliver the least plausible element of the Christian inheritance, salvation from human finitude. Like a frightened child (or like Disney), the capitalist techno-project would simply remove the serpent from Eden for the sake of the happy ending. So naive/arrogant/silly is the pure pursuit of achievable goods, it creates a deeper evil than the impediments to comfort/happiness that it seeks to overcome.

Accordingly, we are left in the apparently absurd position of rendering (c) in our list of alternatives as the credible re-creation of difficulty (in other words outside the aesthetic difficulty advocated by Adorno and outside the recreational violence depicted by J.G. Ballard). Less absurdly, we can call it basic honesty to the case. This responds to the 50-year-old question of Clive Bell: why is it that contemporary Brooklyn, with ample leisure-time, education, funds, sophistication, and so on, is unable to produce a culture as profound as that of the average Italian Renaissance city-state? These towns too were bourgeois, and their principal families were often merchants and bankers; but they were tough towns, not the museum-café-shops that they have become for tourists. Nor does the matter rest on the quality of the art (now occupying two extremes: the unctuous solemnity of major collections and commercial kitsch), but rather upon the depth, seriousness and wit with which human topics could be addressed.

Of course, such towns were smaller than contemporary cities; but the most important difference is that, however fractious among themselves, there was always a deep reservoir of common loyalty in the face of adversity (war, plague, etc.).

Forget therefore any visual imitation of such cities (plenty of that in Dubai already), the issue lies elsewhere. It is addressed by two questions: what is a city for (assuming the answer transcends distribution of goods and the prevention of crime), and does not any version of 'good' city

(an ethical concept) require a basic honesty, or generosity, to the full scope of humanity (one does not get Socrates without the city which killed him).

These two questions point to a more profound issue: a basis for moral judgements (what is good particularly?), and the ethical understanding of what is held in common (what is good universally?). This is of course where all traditional cities started, not from zero but already implicated in a profound commonality symbolised by fractious gods revealed through nature and fate or Plato's Highest Good or God or Allah. Aristotle developed his understanding of the *polis* by building upwards from *ethos* – the fundamental conditions a people held in common.

Since the Enlightenment we have replaced such symbols by valorisation of the subject, who is held to be the source of epistemological certainty and doubt (Descartes), the exponent of self-interest whose aggregate behaviour creates an economy (Adam Smith), the entity whose rights determine law and who is presumed to be the bulwark against tyranny (achieving solidarity in the revolution), and the basis of a purely immanent philosophy (for example, Bourdieu, Badiou, Zizek). We evidently experience our context as a tension between these two modes of self-understanding: between ethos and economics, citizen and crowd, community and statistics, commitments and demographics, depth and surface, tradition and innovation, conditions always already there and possibilities always deferred, intensity and extensity, creativity and invention, language and code, truth and certainty, rootedness and mobility, etc. (This is a tension Le Corbusier captured in his effort to reconcile the temple and the motorcar).

Platitudes like 'global village' aside, it must be admitted that the working understanding of 'global' is currently dominated by economics, in the sense used here. Further, it is safe to assume that no civilisation has been truly sustainable; there were simply fewer people (the population of the whole Roman Empire in the 2nd century was equal to the present population of Great Britain – about 60 million). This is therefore a genuinely new problem, for the present treated mostly within techno-scientific parameters, and therefore still subject to the belief that it can be 'overcome'. Whether through threat of collapse or perspicacity, it seems we are called upon to address what it is we hold in common in a very new way. It is not obvious, for example, that such a thing can be framed for 'delivery' as a 'project' in the familiar manner, but rather needs to take onboard more unorthodox styles of thought, collaborations, representations, practices.

Assuming we will continue to be haunted by the conflict between symbols and technology, we may meanwhile take as our standard or paradigm for the nature of order not any purified Utopia or system, but the messy, conflicted, layered city. This, like Joyce's 'Dear Dirty Dublin', will always involve rogues and saints, cruelty and kindness, misunderstanding, partial understanding, jokes, profound insight, oversight, logos, poetry, mathematics, domes and drains, holy-water and horse-piss.

1. On 29 July 2007
2. *Al-Manakh*, special edition of *Volume*, edited by M. Khoubrou, O. Baumann, R. Koolhaas, 2007, p. 7
3. 'Fear and Money in Dubai', *New Left Review*, 2005
4. *Al-Manakh*, pp. 216–22
5. *Wired* 013, June 2003
6. *All That is Solid Melts into Air: The Experience of Modernity*, Marshall Berman, London Verso, 1982
7. *Al-Manakh*, p. 198

Masterplan of future Dubai, courtesy of Nakheel

BIOGRAPHIES

Amale Andraos
is a co-founder of WORKac — a New York-based firm whose recent projects include a new 35,000-square-foot headquarters for the Diane von Furstenberg Studio and the new masterplan and public space design for the BAM Cultural District in Brooklyn. Ms Andraos was born in Beirut, Lebanon. She has lived in Saudi Arabia, Paris, the Netherlands and Canada, where she received her B.Arch at McGill University. After completing her Master's degree at Harvard University, where she studied with Rem Koolhaas, Ms Andraos moved to the Netherlands to work with OMA and then to New York in 2002. Ms Andraos has taught for several years at the Harvard Graduate School of Design. She is currently professor at Princeton University.

Arup
a global design and business consultancy, the creative force behind many of the world's most innovative and sustainable buildings, transport and civil engineering projects. Arup is a global company with more a quarter of their 9,000 worldwide staff based in Hong Kong and mainland China, where they have operated for more than 30 years. Arup is working on some of the most high-profile projects for the 2008 Beijing Olympic Games: the Olympic Stadium, the National Swimming Centre and the new Terminal 3 at Beijing Capital International Airport.

Pier Vittorio Aureli
is an architect and educator. His studies focus on the relationship between architectural form, political theory and urban history. Aureli teaches at the Berlage Institute and the Architectural Association, and he is visiting professor at Columbia University, and Accademia di Architettura di Mendrisio in Switzerland. Together with Martino Tattara, he is the founder of Dogma.

Shumon Basar
is a London-based writer, editor, curator and educator. He directs the Architectural Association's recently founded Curatorial Practices and Cultural Projects initiative

(AACP), and in 2008 he will co-curate The World of Madelon Vriesendorp there. From 2005 to 2007, he co-curated one of the first Research Clusters at the AA, on the topic of urbanism and politics. He is a contributing editor at *Tank* magazine, columnist at *Blueprint* and *Abitare* and co-editor of *Did Someone Say Participate* (MIT/Revolver) and *With/Without* (Moutamarat/Bidoun).

Peter Carl
teaches design, history and philosophy of architecture at Cambridge University. He believes that architectural and urban order stand as a profound challenge to the several paradigms rooted in systems and information. To this end, he has recently been looking at Pasolini, Bataille and Joyce in the light of Boltzmann and Shannon.

Adina Hempel
is an architect, researcher and photographer who is living in Hamburg. She received her degree in architecture with honours from the Technical University in Dresden in 2006. She was a visiting student at the American University in Sharjah in 2005, where she conducted with Mirco Urban the research project 'Dimension Dubai' on that city's urban development. Hempel also studied at the New York Film Academy and at Columbia University, New York. She won a Scholarship from the Kulturstiftung Dresdner Bank and was nominated for the Kurt-Beyer-Preis in 2006. Currently she is practising as an architect and researching the state of public space and political landscapes.

Kasia Korczak
has been interested in design primarily as a vehicle for producing and distributing content and has increasingly been involved in the publishing end of design. Her work has been exhibited in the Design Museum, London, the Barbican Gallery and Casco, Utrecht. In 2006 she founded the collective Slaves and Tatars with long-time collaborator, artist and writer Payam Sharifi. Under the name What Once Was Korczak collaborates with theoretical physicist Christophe Galfard. She recently

graduated from an MA residency at the Werkplaats Typografie in Arnhem. www.kasia-korczak.com

Neville Mars
has initiated projects that include architecture, urban design, documentaries, art installations, urban research and creative writing. Mars is Creative Director of the Dynamic City Foundation (DCF) in Beijing (www.dynamiccity.org). The first three years of DCF's research in Bejing and North China will be published in December 2007, entitled *The Chinese Dream – A Society Under Construction*. The work will continue to evolve and expand on http://BURB.tv, the world's first open-source design platform dedicated to the understanding and enhancement of China's cities.

Frank van der Salm
is an artist based in Rotterdam, The Netherlands. He has shown at Haunch of Venison, Zürich and the Venice Biennale and most recently in the large-scale survey show at the NAi in Rotterdam, Spectacular City. www.frankvandersalm.com

Slavs and Tatars
is a faction of polemics and intimacies devoted to an area east of the Berlin Wall and west of the Great Wall of China known as Eurasia. Founded by Kasia Korczak and Payam Sharifi, Slavs and Tatars redeems an oft-forgotten, romantic sphere of influence between slavs, caucasians and central asians. www.slavsandtatars.com

Mirco Urban
is an architect, researcher and photographer based in Hamburg. He received his degree in architecture with honours from the Technical University in Dresden in 2006. With Adina Hempel, he was a visiting student at the American University in Sharjah in 2005, where they co-authored the research project 'Dimension Dubai'. He was nominated for the Kurt-Beyer-Preis in 2006. Before moving to Hamburg, Urban lived and worked in Dubai as well as in Basel, Switzerland. His work

has been featured in magazines and books on instant urbanism and 'publicness' in the 21st-century city. He is currently preparing a publication about Dubai and its urban potential.

Boy Vereecken
graduated from the MA programme 'Typography and Research' at Sint-Lucas, Gent, Belgium and is currently on a residency at Werkplaats Typografie, Arnhem, The Netherlands.

COLOPHON

Shumon Basar is deeply grateful to: Katharina Borsi for co-originating the ideas around *Cities from Zero* and for being a perfect co-pioneer in our Cluster foray; the book's generous and always charming contributors; the assiduous group of MA Histories & Theories students who collaborated with us so energetically in the prequel publication *A Document of Scales and/ of Engagement* (2006); to Kasia Korczak and Boy Vereecken for their inspiring graphic wizardry; to Rosa Ainley for her instant language magic; Marilyn Sparrow for patient support; all AA staff who facilitated our Cluster's activities; and the AA Director, Brett Steele, for creating a pedagogical environment predicated on healthy, necessary renewal and experiment.

Editor
Shumon Basar
Graphic Design
Kasia Korczak & Boy Vereecken
Editorial assistance
Rosa Ainley

This book is based around a Symposium held at Architectural Association on 10 November 2006, organised through the Architectural Urbanism, Social and Political Space Research Cluster, which was curated by Shumon Basar and Katharina Borsi from 2005 to 2007.

AA Publications are initiated by the Director of the AA School, Brett Steele.
publications@aaschool.ac.uk

Printed at Roos en Roos, Arnhem, NL

ISBN 978-1-902902-60-9

Founded in 1847, the AA is the UK's only independent school of architecture, offering undergraduate, postgraduate and research degrees in architecture and related fields.

For further information visit
www.aaschool.ac.uk

AA School of Architecture
36 Bedford Square
London WC1B 3ES
Telephone +44 (0)20 7887 4021
Fax +44 (0)20 7414 0783